Y0-AAH-013

RSVP: THE DIRECTORY OF ILLUSTRATION & DESIGN IS PUBLISHED BY RICHARD LEBENSON AND KATHLEEN CREIGHTON, P.O. BOX 314, BROOKLYN, N.Y. 11205 • VOL.18, NO.1 • ISBN # 1-878118-02-1

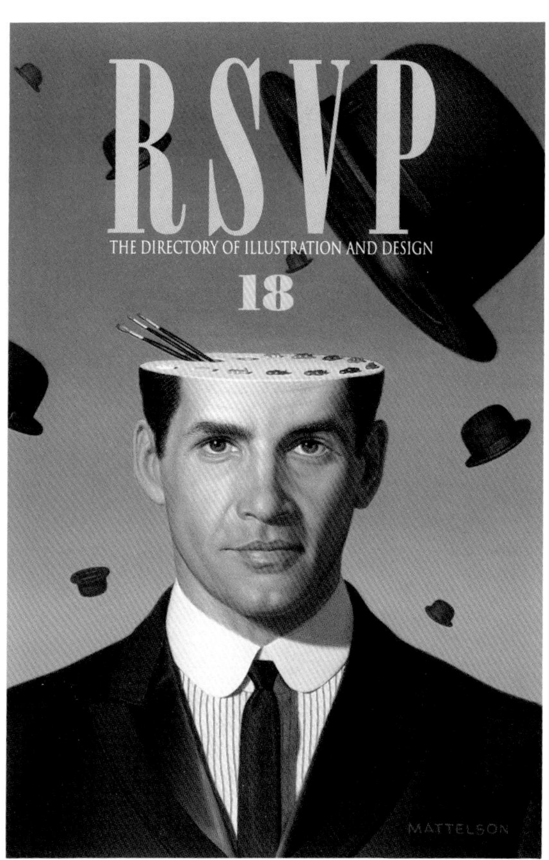
RSVP
THE DIRECTORY OF ILLUSTRATION AND DESIGN
18
MATTELSON

RSVP 18: AN ILLUSTRATOR IN NYC AND AN ART DIRECTOR IN DENVER...WORKING TOGETHER ON AN ANIMATED AD FOR MCDONALDS. AN ARTIST IN GEORGIA WORKING ON A NATIONAL ACCOUNT...FOR NIKE IN PORTLAND, OREGON. A SERIES OF POSTERS FOR THE UTAH SHAKESPEARE FESTIVAL, EXECUTED BY AN ARTIST IN QUEENS, NY. ALL EXAMPLES OF WHAT WE DO BEST. WE PUT PEOPLE IN TOUCH.

WE'VE BEEN CALLED "A POCKETFUL OF VISUAL MIRACLES," AND THAT SUMS US UP VERY NICELY. EXCITING AND STIMULATING ASSIGNMENTS, USING EVERY STYLE, TECHNIQUE AND CONCEPT IMAGINABLE.

MOST OF ALL WE'RE EASY TO USE AND INFORMATIVE. WE KEEP YOU IN TOUCH WITH ARTISTS AND REPS THROUGH RSVP CALLBACK® (718) 857-9267. AND WE TAKE MESSAGES AND UPDATE YOU ABOUT ANY ARTIST IN THE BOOK. SO, GIVE US A CALL. AND ENJOY RSVP18.

PUBLISHER: RICHARD LEBENSON & KATHLEEN CREIGHTON • **COORDINATION/ SALES**: RICHARD LEBENSON • **DESIGN & PROMOTION**: KATHLEEN CREIGHTON & STEPHEN BODKIN • **BUSINESS & PROMOTION**: JOE GREENSTEIN • **OFFICE MANAGER**: HARVEY WILSON • **SALES**: PAUL KRAUSS • **TRAFFIC**: FRANK ATTONG • **TYPESETTING**: BRAINCHILD DESIGNS • **PRODUCTION**: JOHN CLEVELAND • **COVER ILLUSTRATION**: MARVIN MATTELSON • **COVER DESIGN**: RICHARD BLEIWEISS • **SPECIAL THANKS**: TOMMASO GIANNOTTA, TONY BRUSCO, AL DE ANGELO, JUAN HUNT, WINSTON JOHN, CARLOS ORTIZ, HERB ROSIN, GARY STAHL, **PRINTING**: FLEETWOOD LITHO

CREDITS

RSVP 18 FEATURES THE WORK OF 245 ARTISTS, ILLUSTRATORS AND DESIGNERS NATIONWIDE • INDEXED ALPHABETICALLY BY SPECIFIC SKILLS, AND BY REGION IN OUR GEOGRAPHIC INDEX • RSVP CALLBACK® 718/857-9267, OUR 24 HOUR, 7 DAY/WEEK ANSWERING SERVICE • (SEE PAGE 304 FOR COMPLETE DETAILS)

ILLUSTRATION

COLOR...13

BLACK & WHITE...233

DESIGN

COLOR...220

BLACK & WHITE...275

INDEX..290

GEOGRAPHIC INDEX..............................300

CONTENTS

RSVP18'S COVER ARTIST MARVIN MATTELSON'S AWARD-WINNING WORK COMBINES A HIGHLY FOCUSED REALISM WITH A STRONG DESIGN SENSE, TO CREATE SURREAL AND STRAIGHT FORWARD IMAGES THAT HAVE GREAT VITALITY AND POWER. BORN IN PHILADELPHIA, HE ARRIVED IN NEW YORK TO PURSUE A CAREER IN ILLUSTRATION AFTER GRADUATING FROM THE PHILADELPHIA COLLEGE OF ART.

MARVIN'S WORK HAS BEEN SEEN WORLDWIDE. HIS CLIENTS INCLUDE: IBM, LINCOLN MERCURY, ABC, THE ARTS & ENTERTAINMENT NETWORK, TIME-WARNER, NEWSWEEK, AT&T, ITT, NYNEX, PENTHOUSE, PLAYBOY, NATIONAL GEOGRAPHIC, LIFE, METROPOLITAN LIFE, AND SVA. HE RESIDES IN GREAT NECK, NY WITH HIS WIFE AND AGENT, JUDY MATTELSON AND THEIR SONS, ERIC AND MICHAEL.

ILLUSTRATION

ALAN REINGOLD

ANITA GRIEN-REPRESENTING ARTISTS
155 EAST 38 STREET, NEW YORK, NEW YORK 10016 (212) 697-6170

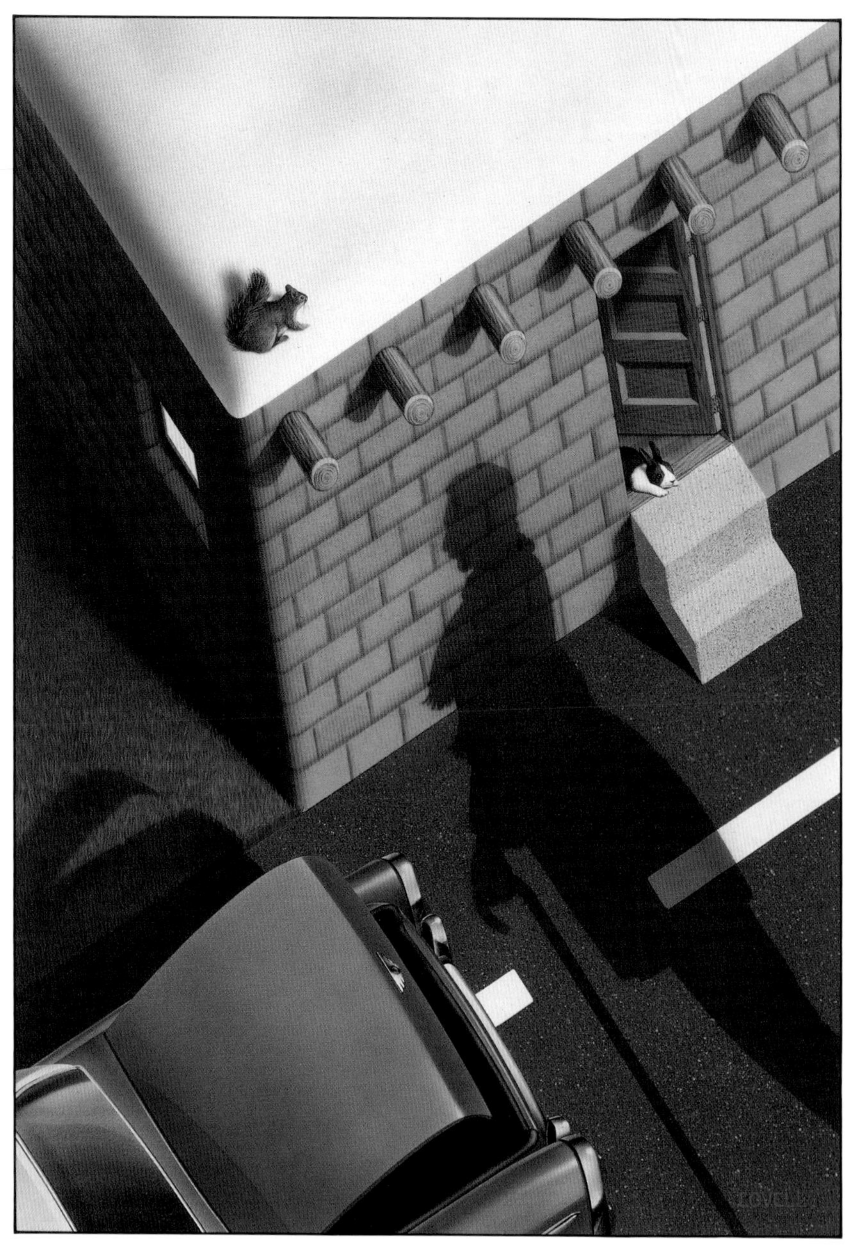

R I C K   L O V E L L

2860 LAKEWIND COURT • ALPHARETTA, GA 30302
404 • 442 • 3943 FAX 404 • 475 • 8321

SEE RSVP 16 AND 17 TO SEE MORE OF MY WORK.

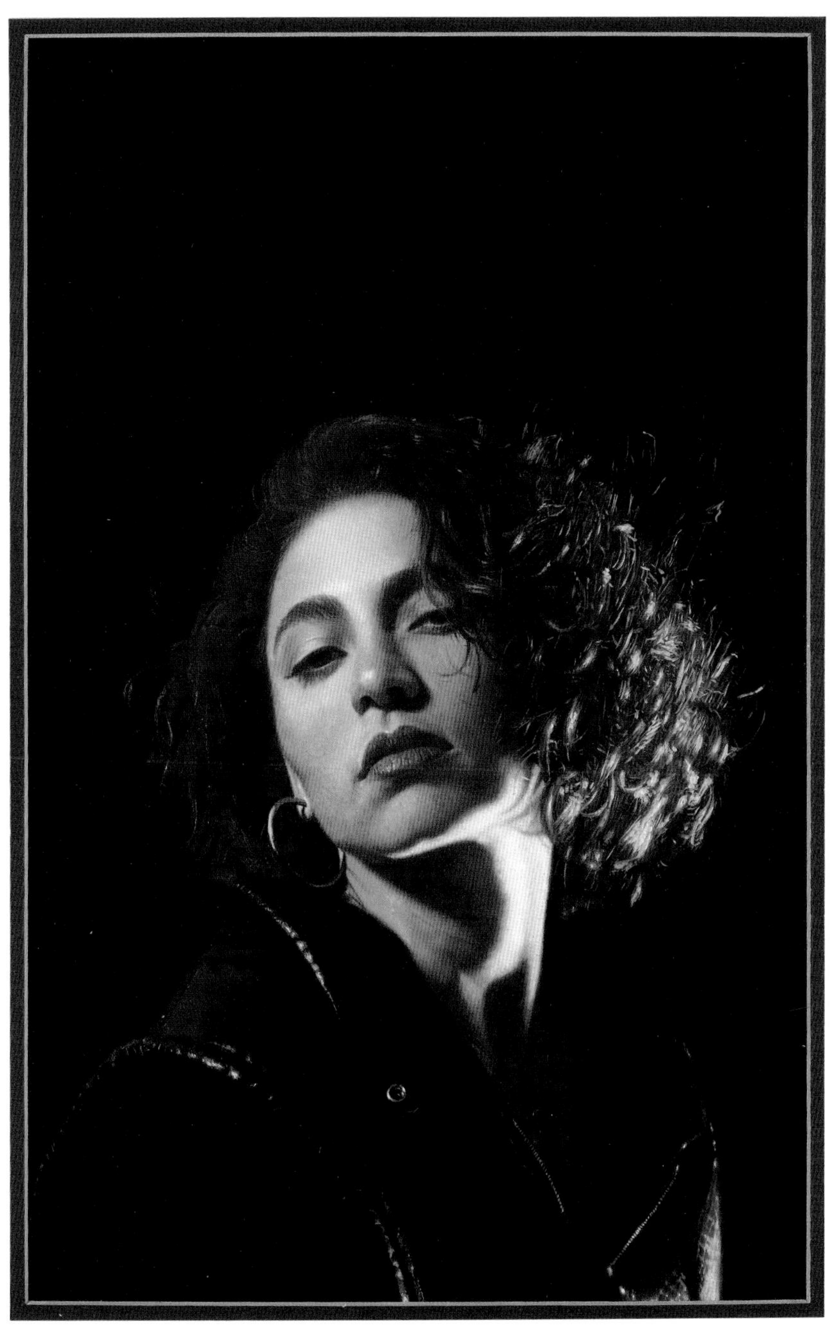

MATTHEW ARCHAMBAULT (516) 277-4722
127 WIDGEON CT., GREAT RIVER, N.Y. 11739

JOHN STEVEN GURNEY

PHONE/FAX (718) 462–5073, RSVP CALLBACK (718) 857–9267

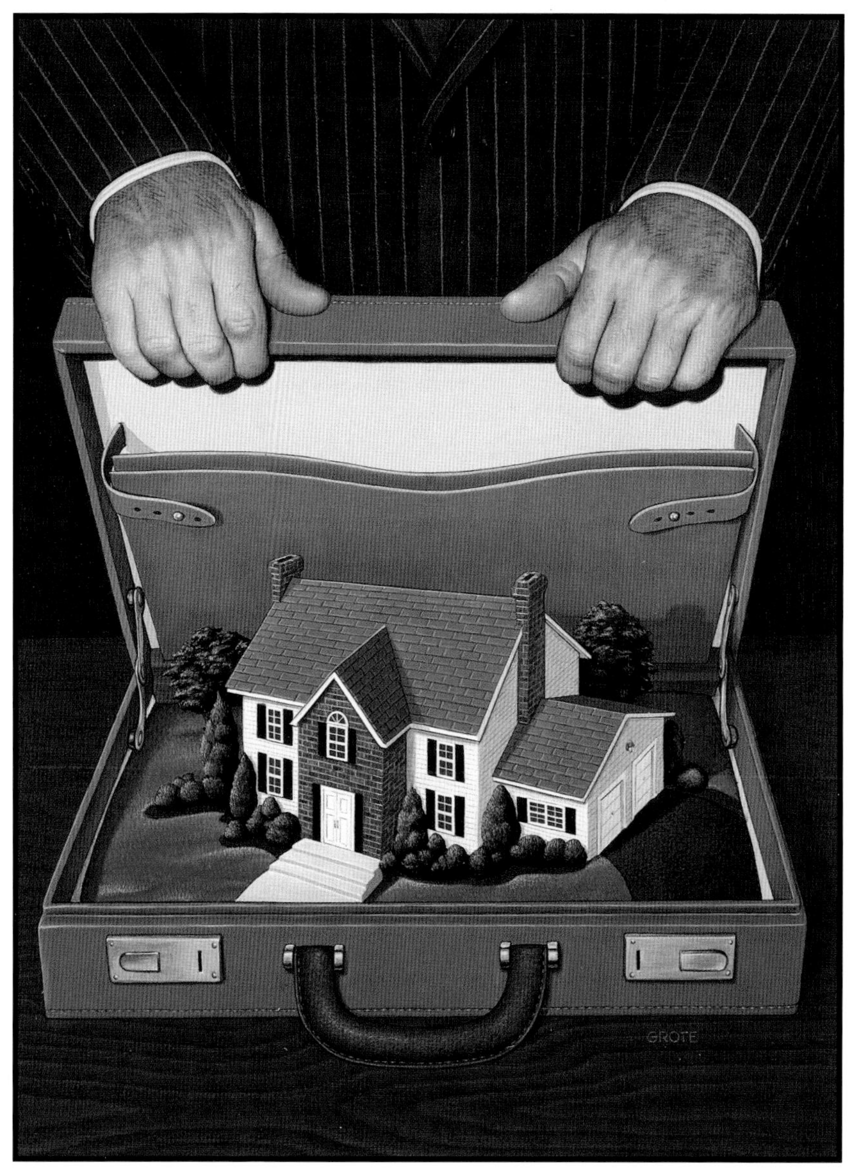

R I C H G R O T E

609-586-5896

21 TYNDALE RD., HAMILTON SQUARE, NEW JERSEY 08690
• CALL FOR FAX NUMBER •

Jill Bauman / Illustrator

p. o. box 152, jamaica, n.y. 11415 (718) 886~5616

WALTER VELEZ / ILLUSTRATOR

REPRESENTED BY JILL BAUMAN
(718)886-5616

Illustrator
DON IVAN PUNCHATZ
2605 Westgate Dr.
Arlington, Texas 76015
(817) 469 - 8151 metro

Represented by
DARWIN BAHM
6 Jane St.
New York, NY 10014
(212) 989 - 7074

BOB BAHM
4191 Pearl Rd.
Cleveland, Ohio 44109
(216) 398 - 1338

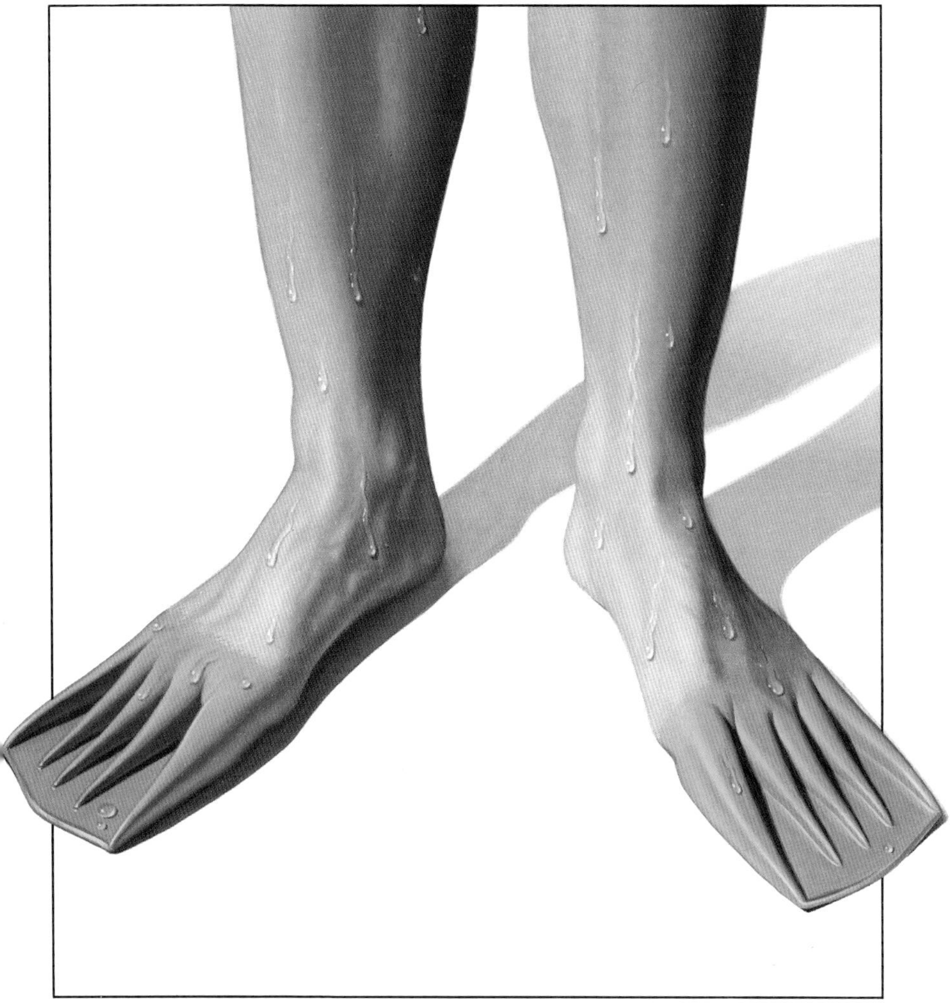

MARVIN MATTELSON

Anthony Valentino Robinson
Humorous Illustration

RSVP CALLBACK ANSWERING SERVICE (718) 857–9267

157 CLINTON STREET, BROOKLYN HEIGHTS, NY 11201
TEL: (718) 875–3236

MARK
F R E D R I C K S O N
6 0 2 - 7 2 2 - 5 7 7 7

Mark Fredrickson • 853 S. Pantano Parkway • Tucson, Arizona 85710 • 602-722-5777

R. MARTIN

RICHARD MARTIN, P.O.BOX 268, WANTAGH, NY 11793
(516) 377-3844

Jim DeLapine

AIRBRUSHED ILLUSTRATION
(516) 225-1247
398 31ST STREET, LINDENHURST, NEW YORK 11757

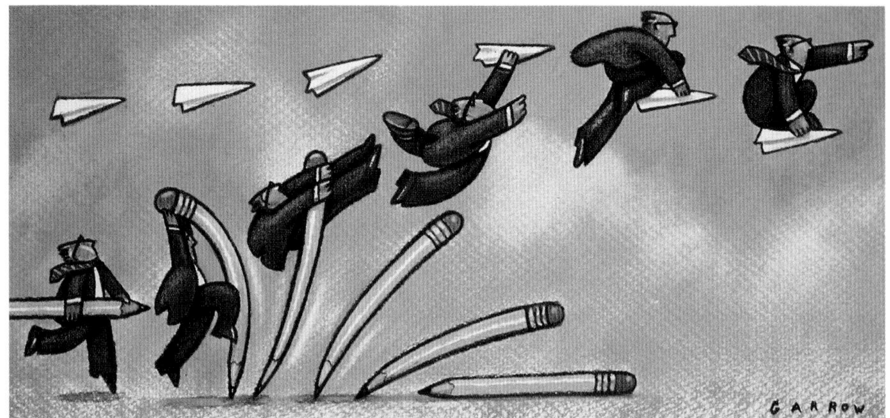

DAN GARROW

Renard Represents • tel(212)490-2450 • fax(212)697-6828

KAZUHIKO SANO

Renard Represents • tel (212) 490-2450 • fax (212) 697-6828

JAMES BOZZINI

Renard Represents • tel (212) 490-2450 • fax (212) 697-6828

TOM ROBERTS
P.O. BOX 283, BUDD LAKE, NJ 07828
(201) 347-7743

ANDY LACKOW
7004 BOULEVARD EAST 29C • GUTTENBERG, NJ 07093 • 201-854-2770

ROBERT ROPER

JAMES BERNARDIN
ILLUSTRATION

531 4TH AVENUE SOUTH, UNIT 6, EDMONDS, WA 98020
(206) 771-1348

HODGES
SOILEAU
ILLUSTRATION
203·852·0751
350 FLAX HILL RD. NORWALK CT 06854
• FAX 203 • 831 • 9155 •

Rodney Jung

67–14 108TH ST., 2A, FOREST HILLS, N.Y. 11375
(718) 544–4278 FAX (718) 544–3341

SMART ART

HIGH CONCEPT HUMOR

The Risks of Faxpionage *American Management Association*

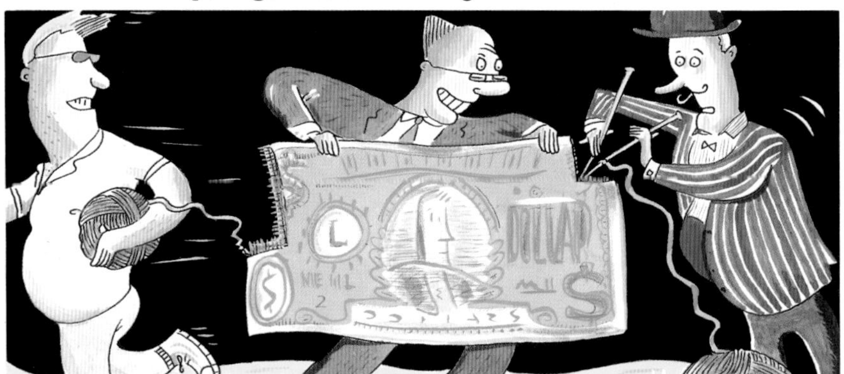

Lloyds of London Insures Deferred Compensation *BusinessWeek*

CLIENTS INCLUDE: NEWSWEEK, TIME–WARNER, PIZZA HUT, OGILVY & MATHER, ARTHUR D. LITTLE, SESAME STREET, DOW JONES, U.S.A. TODAY, N.Y. TIMES, BOSTON GLOBE, E.D.S. CORP., ET. AL.

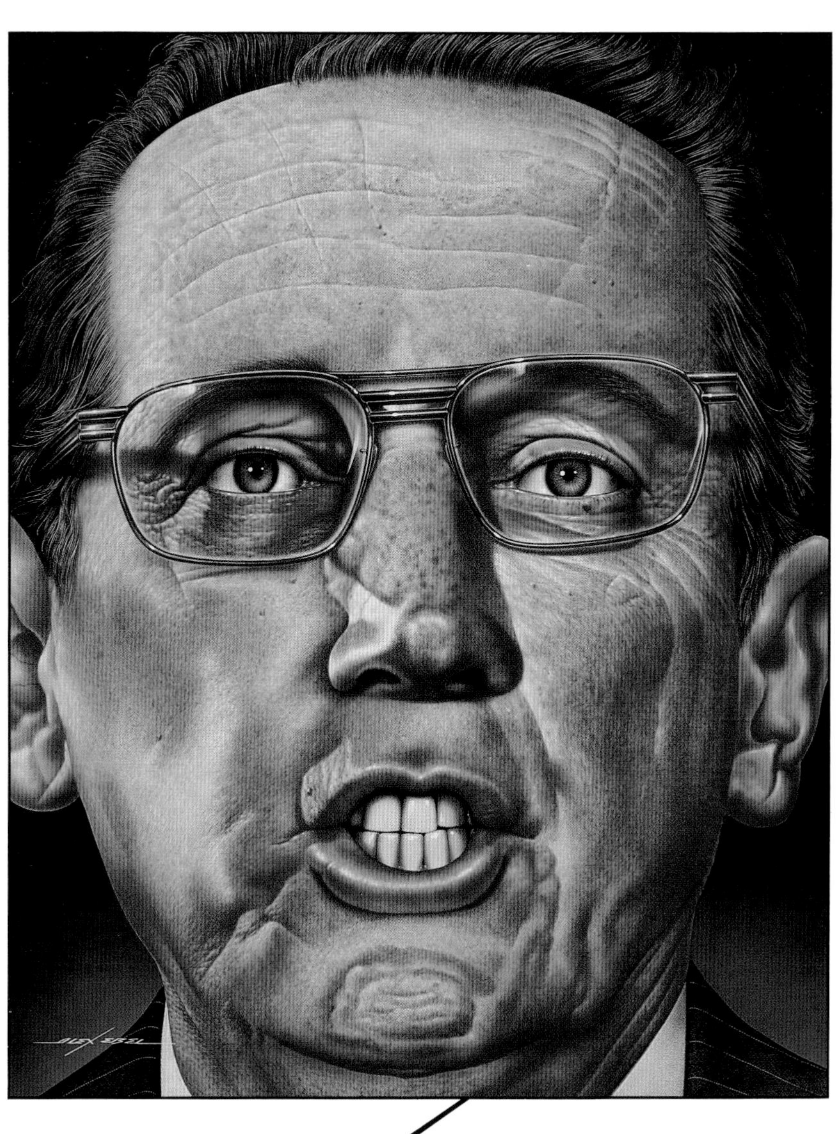

ALEX EBEL

30 NEWPORT ROAD, YONKERS, NEW YORK 10710 (914) 961–4058

MIKE LESTER
illustration
(706) 234-7733
FAX (706) 234-7594

DAVID MILGRIM ILLUSTRATION

NEW YORK CITY
(212) 673–1432, CALL TO SEE MORE.

MARY LEMPA 708•447•4454 FAX: 708•447•0301

RON BARRETT WORKS OF HUMOR
2112 BROADWAY, NEW YORK CITY, N.Y. 10023
(212) 874 •1370

WENDELL
M·I·N·O·R
15 OLD NORTH RD
P O BOX 1135
WASHINGTON, CT
ZIP 06793
203 868-9101
FAX 868-9512

CAMERON CLEMENT
NATIONAL GRAPHIC EXPLORER
918/621/5261

CLIFFORD FAUST

NEW YORK CITY (212) 581-9461
RSVP CALLBACK ANSWERING SERVICE (718) 857-9267

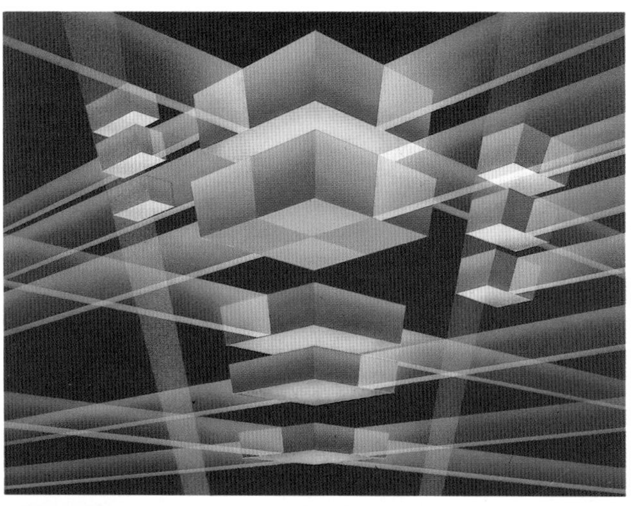

◄ *Communications of the ACM*

Salem Krieger

CLIENTS

AT&T
McGraw Hill Publishing
McMillan Publishing
Saatchi & Saatchi, New York
VNR Publishing
W.H. Freeman Publishers
Ziff Davis

◄ *Padomar Yachts, Inc. Greece*

91 PARK AVENUE, HOBOKEN, N.J. 07030
PHONE 201 •963 •3754 • FAX 201 •963 •3754

DAVID BRION
28 CHEEVER PLACE, BROOKLYN, NY 11231
(718) 858-0362 • FAX (718) 596-4408

LANE DUPONT 203 • 222 • 1562
20 EVERGREEN AVE • WESTPORT, CT 06880

illustration by

MICHAEL SOURS

TRUDY SANDS • ARTIST REPRESENTATIVE • 214/905-9037
1350 CHEMICAL STREET, DALLAS, TX 75207 FAX: 214/905-9038

TIM McCLURE

Trudy Sands
ARTIST REPRESENTATIVE

214-905-9037 • FAX 214-905-9038

1350 CHEMICAL STREET, DALLAS, TX 75207

Art from Photo © Mark Kozlowski, 1982"

SHOW AND TELL, HOLIDAY HOUSE

DENISE BRUNKUS
SILVERPIN STUDIO/ILLUSTRATION
(908) 735-2671

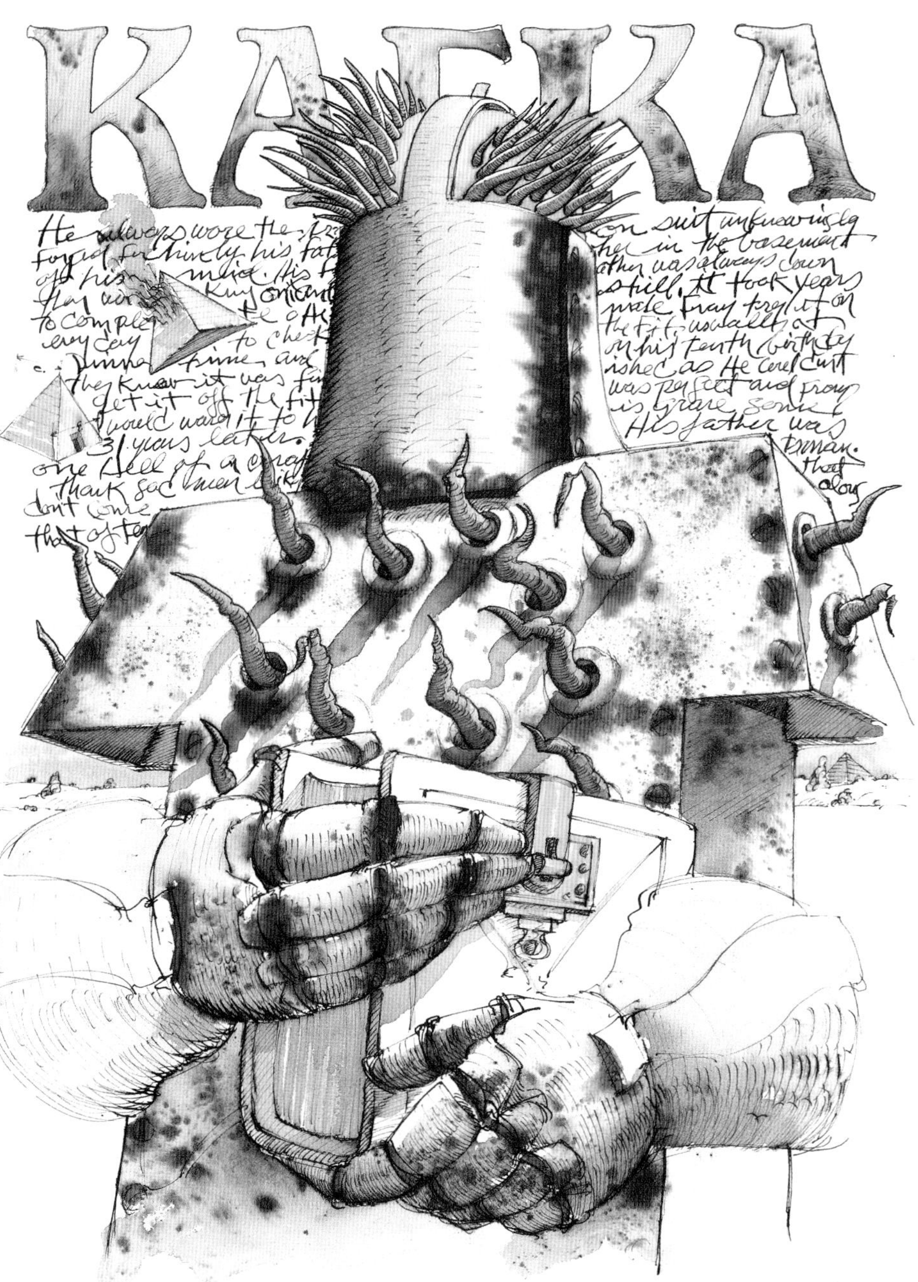
KAFKA
BOB CONGE 716-473-0291

GOODYEAR
© K. Spangler 92

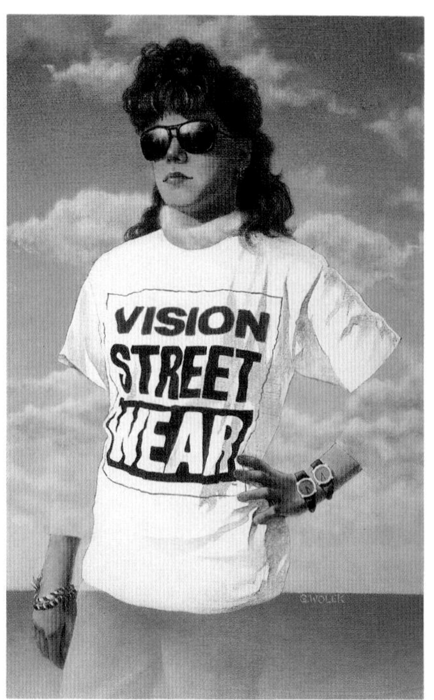

GUY WOLEK

ILLUSTRATION • (918) 451-2546

EDWARD ABRAMS

REPRESENTED BY DAVID SCROGGY
PHONE • 619 • 544 • 9571
FAX • 619 • 544 • 0743

RICK GEARY

REPRESENTED BY DAVID SCROGGY
PHONE • 619 • 544 • 9571
FAX • 619 • 544 • 0743

LIONEL TALARO

REPRESENTED BY DAVID SCROGGY
PHONE • 619 • 544 • 9571
FAX • 619 • 544 • 0743

ANGELO

ARTIST/ILLUSTRATOR EXTRAORDINAIRE
1449 LONGFELLOW AVENUE, BRONX, NY 10459
(718) 617-2907, RSVP CALLBACK ANSWERING SERVICE (718) 857-9267

JIM HARTER
FINE COLLAGE ILLUSTRATION
RSVP CALLBACK ANSWERING SERVICE (718) 857–9267

DOROTHY REINHARDT

415•584•9369

SCRATCHBOARD AND WATERCOLOR
466 MELROSE AVE., SAN FRANCISCO, CALIFORNIA 94127
RSVP CALLBACK ANSWERING SERVICE (718) 857–9267

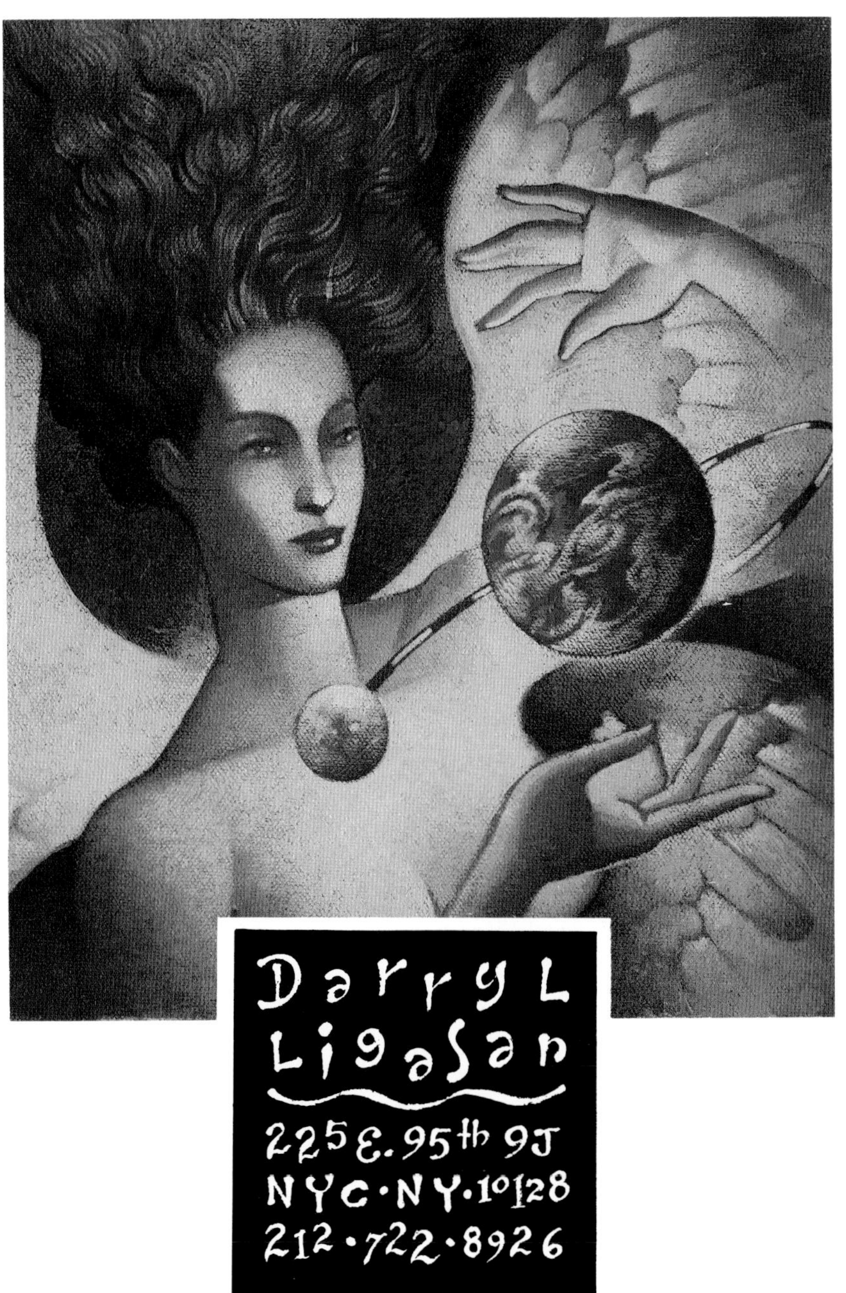

RSVP CALLBACK ANSWERING SERVICE (718) 857–9267

G R E G O R Y   H E R G E R T

RSVP CALLBACK ANSWERING SERVICE (718) 857–9267

CHRIS MILES • ILLUSTRATION
(718) 499–1656
RSVP CALLBACK ANSWERING SERVICE (718) 857–9267

ERGO, ERGO

That ever present god of work ***ERGON*** is breathing down your neck. Driving, grinding, forcing you to create perfection. I can make your illustration worries less stressful!

Chuck Galey / *Humorous Illustration*
(Therefore, I work)
601.373.6426

Appease the gods! To receive monthly calendars with ***ERGON's*** family of work demi-gods, give me a call!

REPRESENTED BY ANDREA LYNCH/REPERTOIRE: 214•369•6990
SEE CREATIVE ILLUSTRATION '90, PG. 130 FOR MORE SAMPLES

B.K. Taylor

24940 S.CROMWELL, FRANKLIN, MI 48025 (313) 626-8698 FAX (313) 855-8247
IN NY CONTACT IVY MINDLIN, IVY LEAGUE OF ARTISTS
156 FIFTH AVENUE, NEW YORK, NY 10010 (212) 243-1333

S.B.WHITEHEAD ILLUSTRATION

200 E.27TH STREET #5C • NEW YORK, N.Y. 10016
(TEL) 212 • 686 • 5250 • 718 • 768 • 0803 • (FAX) 212 • 686 • 5624 CLIENTS:
AT&T • TIME/WARNER • NFL • READER'S DIGEST • SIMON & SCHUSTER • ARISTA RECORDS

STEPHEN SWENY

310·823·0095

RSVP CALLBACK (718) 857–9267

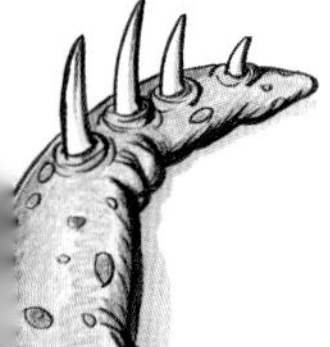

TRAVEL
ROBERT ZIMMERMAN
Telephone: 718-237-0699

MUSIC

John is my kinda guy. N shower, Mindy, Charlie, Barbara and McCauley are for dinner. Debby and Lucy might make it as well.Insert few bold lines odummy copy get the reader going. Make to the point, dum dummy cop close behi dummy copy the night Dean Barb Betts, Joe Lewis Du Von

Shannon Wilkinson, Nancy Chris Sloan, Cynthia Frie Judy Tillinger, Richard A Jay Petrow, Bar Anderson, Joe Yacir Alice Cook, Mer Mayer, Lisa Ors Vince LaMonte, Do Kogan, Nan Strengold, Ke Kleppert, Robb Alle Melissa Jacoby Another smashing paragraph of dummy copy needs to go right here. This dummy copy will glue the reader to the page. Dummy copy like this don't come along every day.Thanks Kathy Cacchione, Elin Von

illustation to accompany this dummy copy. A dummy illustrator will be hired d forced to read this dummy copy and e up with a dummy idea. ... is an artist. Pete Thorpe is one. Mark Matcho is an genius. Mike Bartalos will to play a guitar. I talked to s once on the telephone. He was guy. Lila is my little fruit cake.

Spreckelson, Catie Aldrich, Peter Deutsch, Greg Akiyama, Debby Racano, Andy Hall, Peter Gould, Kitty McGee, Kaie Wellman, John Cavea, Cathy Caldwell, John Belknap, David Herbick, Victor Chan, Fred Lind, Horst Weber, Michael Kaye, Joe Dizney, Steven Taylor, Nichole White, Sheri Olmon, John Liegy, Angela Miller, Clay Smith, Doug Grimmit, Anne Ray, Jim Briggs. This ad designed by my friend Jay Petrow.

PHILIP A. SCHEUER
126 FIFTH AVENUE, NY, NY 10011 (212) 620 • 0728
SEE RSVP 11–17, AMERICAN SHOWCASE 15, CREATIVE ILLUS. 1993

KIMBLE

KIMBLE PENDLETON MEAD
125 PROSPECT PARK WEST, BROOKLYN, NY 11215
(718) 768–3632

SHARON WATTS
201 EASTERN PARKWAY • BROOKLYN, NY • 11238
718•398•0451

STEVE HENRY
7 PARK AVENUE, NEW YORK, N.Y. 10016
(212) 532–2487

ROBIN OLIMB OLIMB GRAFIX **(619) 566-6247**

PAPER SCULPTURE • WHIMSICAL CARTOONS
11454 ELBERT WAY • SAN DIEGO, CA 92126 • FAX (619) 566-3528

DAN V. ROMER

176 FIFTH AVENUE #4R, BROOKLYN, NEW YORK 11217
(718) 789-8442

MENA DOLOBOWSKY

REPRESENTED BY HELEN ROMAN ASSOCIATES
1-800-472-2047 203-222-1608 FAX AVAILABLE

XII
Le Pendu
MARZIA

WE DO NOT SEE NATURE WITH OUR EYES, BUT WITH OUR UNDERSTANDING AND OUR HEARTS.
William Hazlitt
APRIL BLAIR STEWART
REPRESENTED BY HELEN ROMAN ASSOCIATES
1-800-472-2047 203-222-1608 FAX AVAILABLE

SERGE MICHAELS 11435 EMELITA ST. #1 NORTH HOLLYWOOD, CA 91601 818 / 753-1453

GATEWAY FOR AN INGÉNUE

Vincent Amicosante

VINCENT AMICOSANTE

4 0 8 • 4 7 9 • 4 8 0 3

511 Sunset Drive, Capitola by the Sea, California 95010

• RSVP CALLBACK ANSWERING SERVICE • 718 • 857 • 9267 •

Scott Roberts Illustrator

28 WEST 25TH STREET, BALTIMORE, MD 21218 (410) 366-0737

KATHLEEN E. CREIGHTON, PHOTOGRAPHIC ILLUSTRATION
718.636.1111/857.9267

Kathleen E. Creighton
photographic illustration
718.636.1111/857.9267

FRANK R. SOFO

16 BRANCH LANE, LEVITTOWN, N.Y. 11756 (516) 681-8745
RSVP CALLBACK ANSWERING SERVICE (718) 857-9267

MARK TEXEIRA

188 MIDLAND AVE, TUCKAHOE, N.Y. 10707 (914) 337–2286
RSVP CALLBACK ANSWERING SERVICE (718) 857–9267

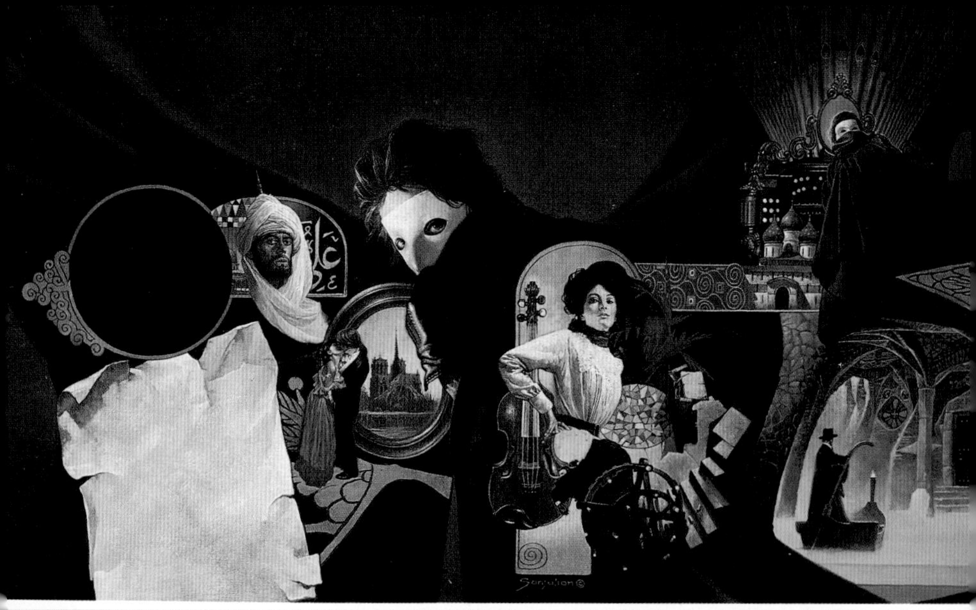

S A N J U L I A N

S.I. International · (212) 254-4996 · Fax (212) 995-0911
RSVP Callback Answering Service (718) 857-9267

E N R I C

S.I. International • (212) 254-4996 • Fax (212) 995-0911
RSVP Callback Answering Service (718) 857-9267

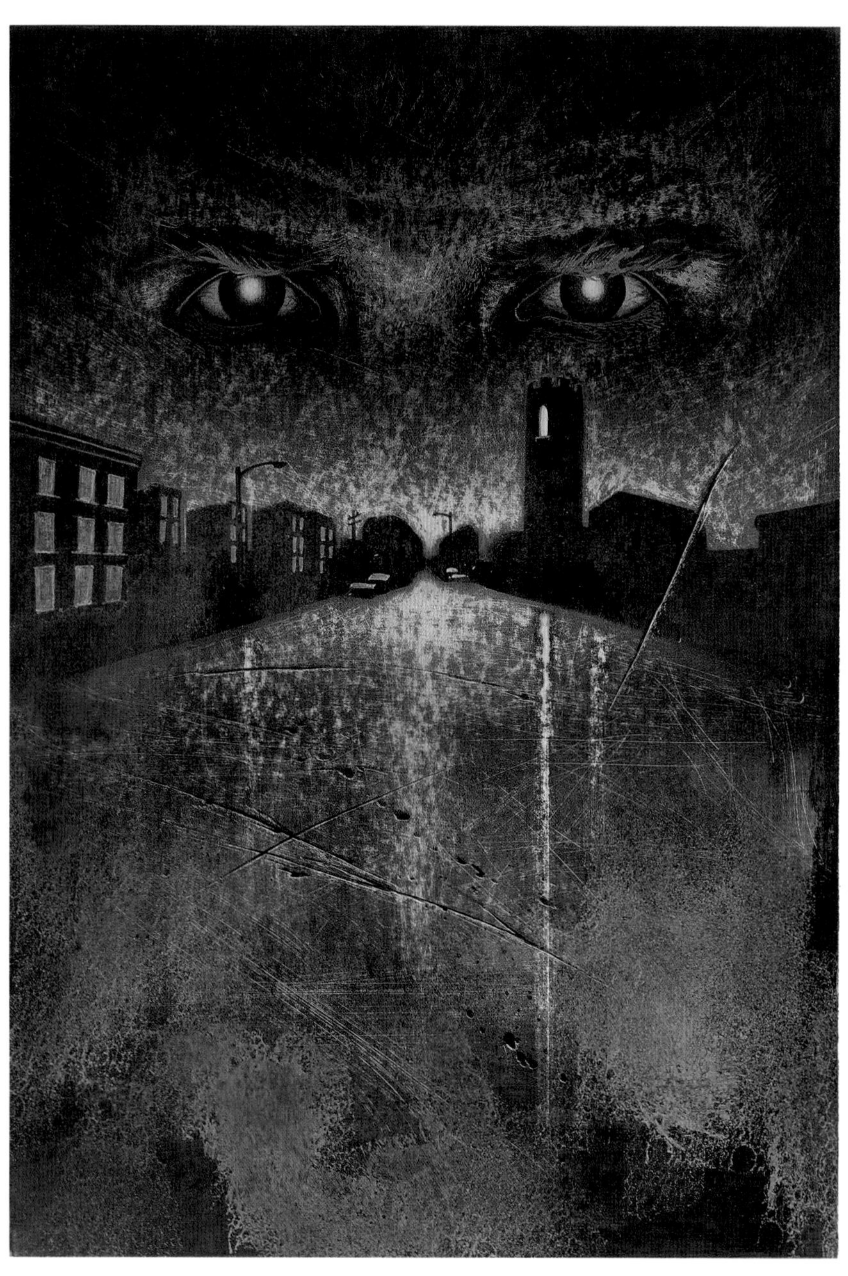

J I M · D E A L

S.I. International · (212) 254-4996 · Fax (212) 995-0911
RSVP Callback Answering Service (718) 857-9267

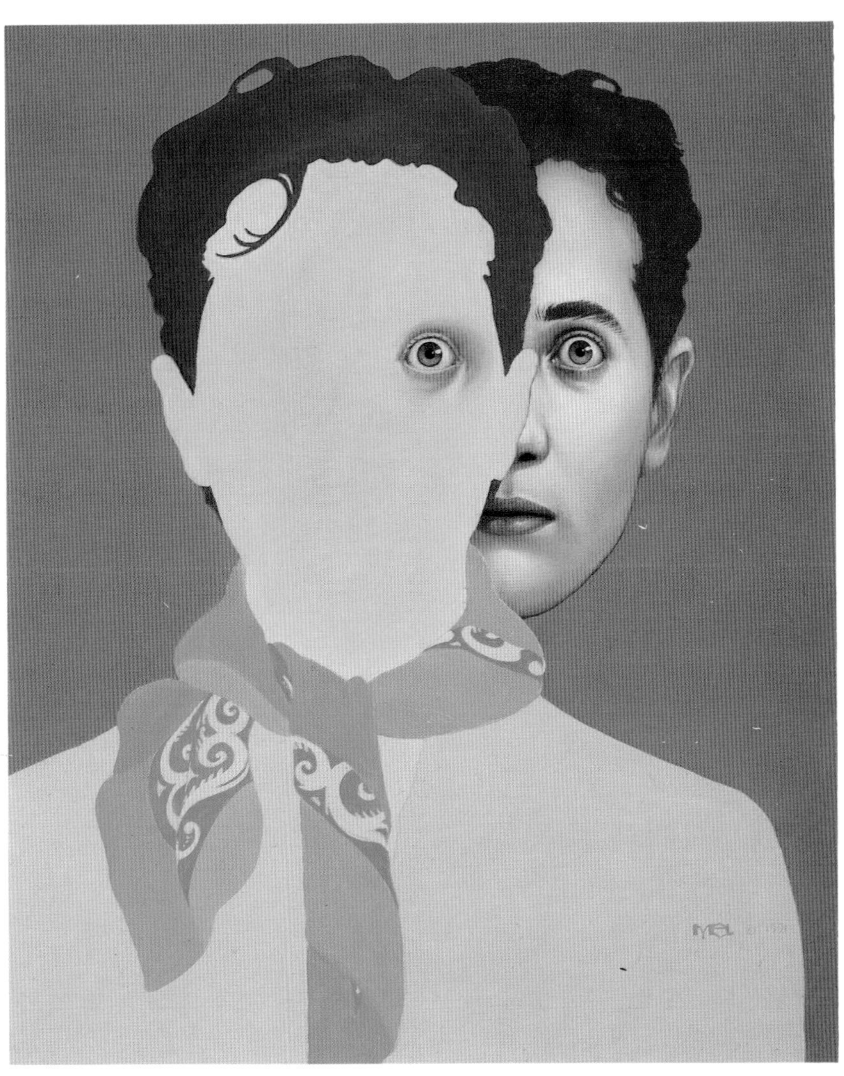

M E L · G R A N T

S.I. International · (212) 254-4996 · Fax (212) 995-0911
RSVP Callback Answering Service (718) 857-9267

S T E V E · H A E F E L E

S.I. International · (212) 254-4996 · Fax (212) 995-0911
RSVP Callback Answering Service (718) 857-9267

F R E D · M A R V I N

S.I. International · (212) 254-4996 · Fax (212) 995-0911
RSVP Callback Answering Service (718) 857-9267

T O M · L A P A D U L A

S.I. International · (212) 254-4996 · Fax (212) 995-0911
RSVP Callback Answering Service (718) 857-9267

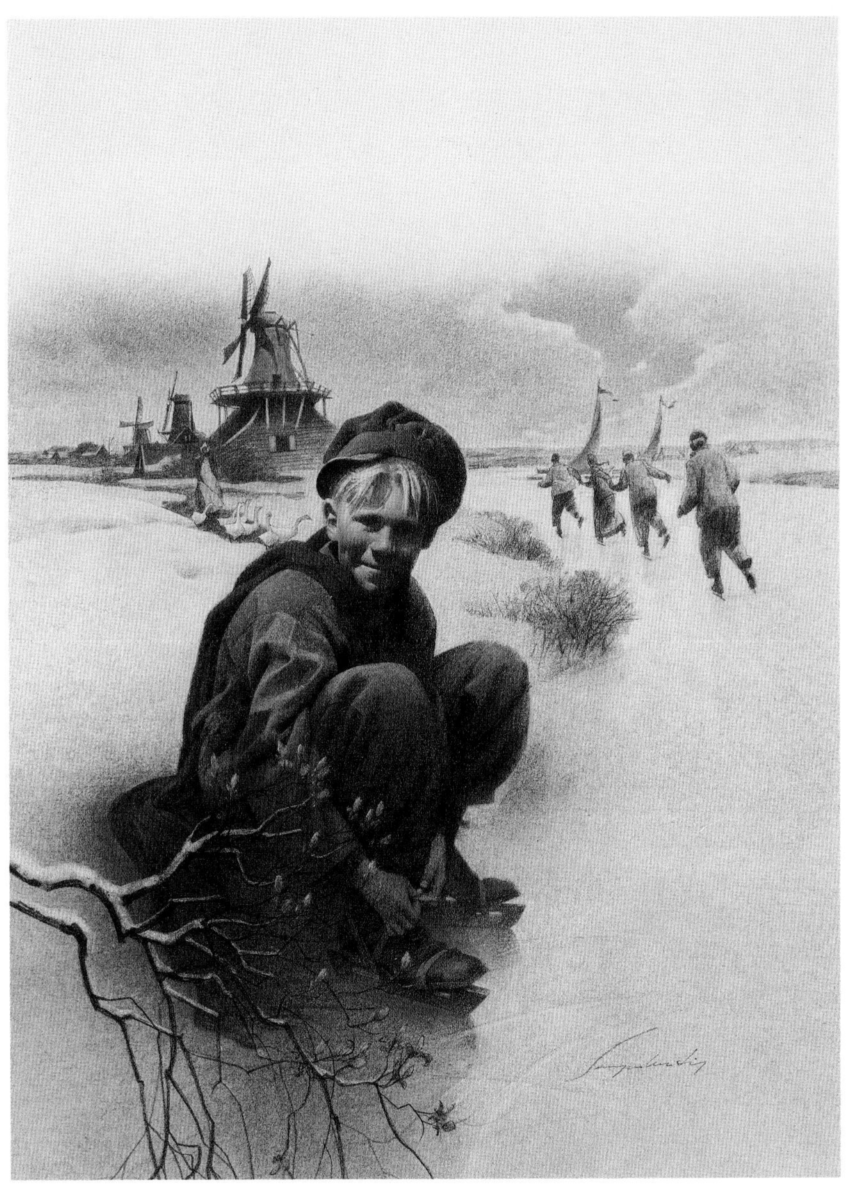

SERGIO • MARTINEZ

S.I. International • (212) 254-4996 • Fax (212) 995-0911
RSVP Callback Answering Service (718) 857-9267

H O L L Y · H A N N O N

S.I. International · (212) 254-4996 · Fax (212) 995-0911
RSVP Callback Answering Service (718) 857-9267

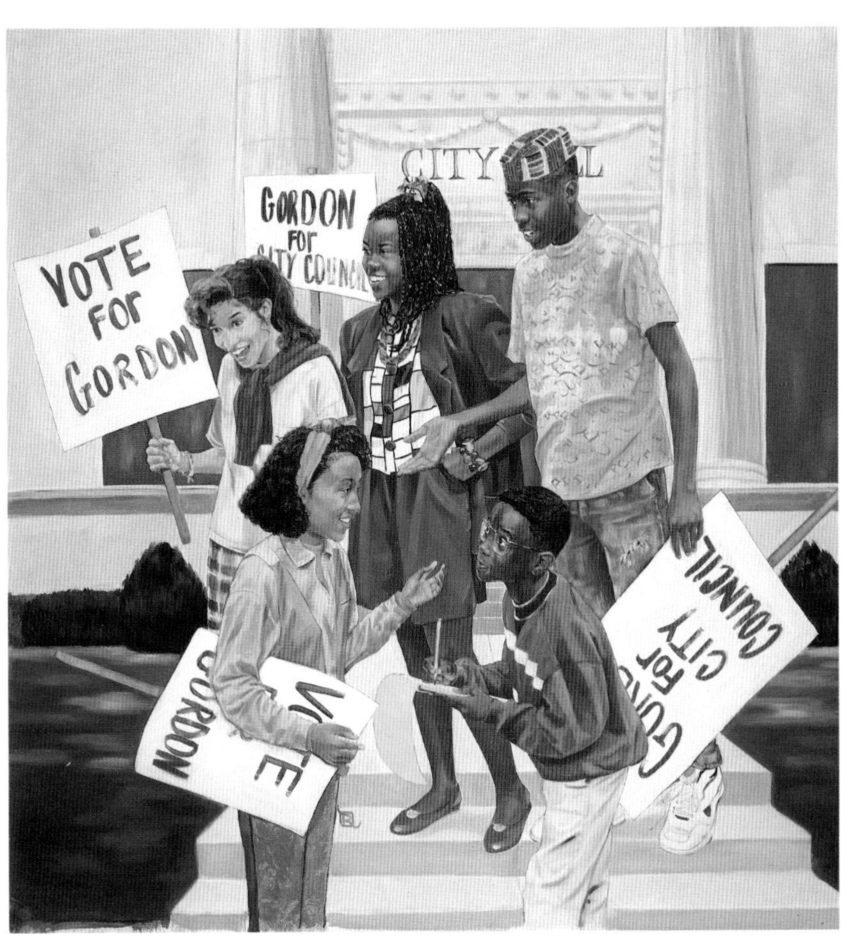

MELODYE · ROSALES

S.I. International · (212) 254-4996 · Fax (212) 995-0911
RSVP Callback Answering Service (718) 857-9267

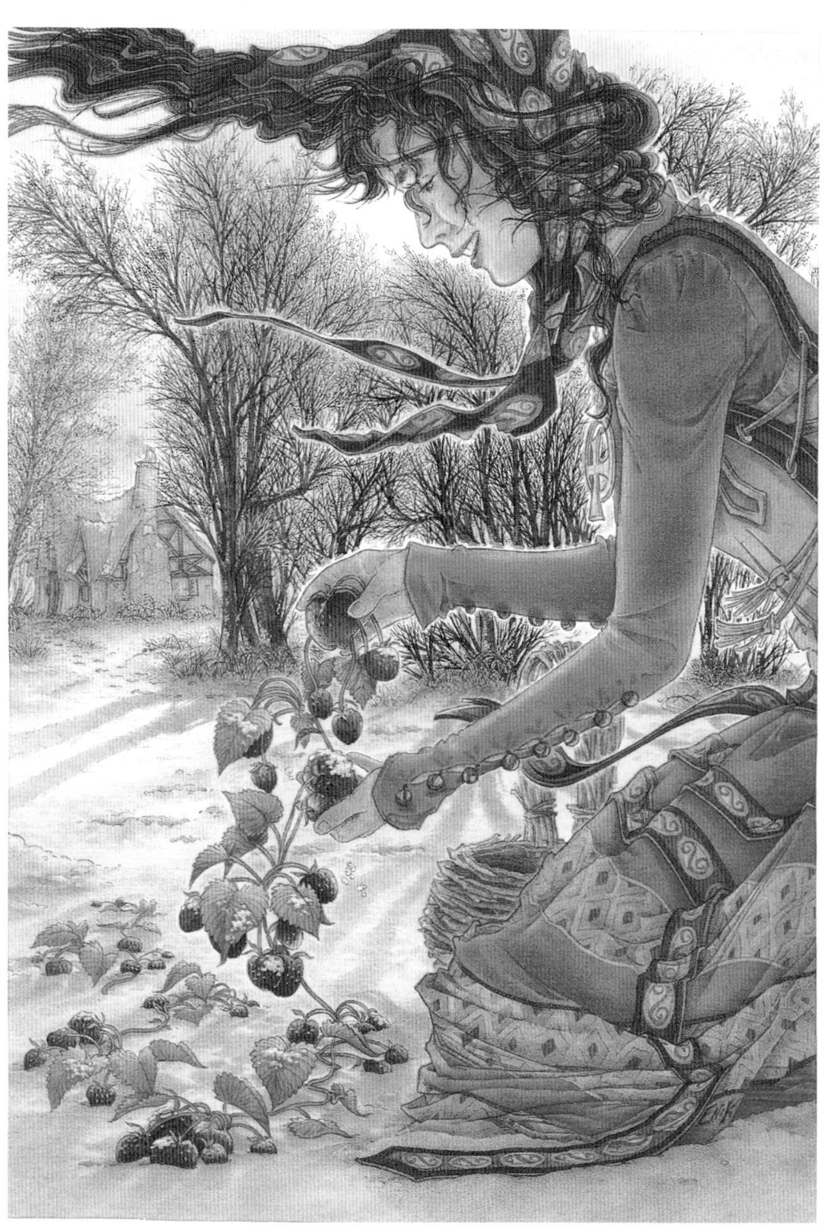

T E D • E N I K

S.I. International • (212) 254-4996 • Fax (212) 995-0911
RSVP Callback Answering Service (718) 857-9267

CAROLYN • BRACKEN

S.I. International • (212) 254-4996 • Fax (212) 995-0911
RSVP Callback Answering Service (718) 857-9267

THOMPSON

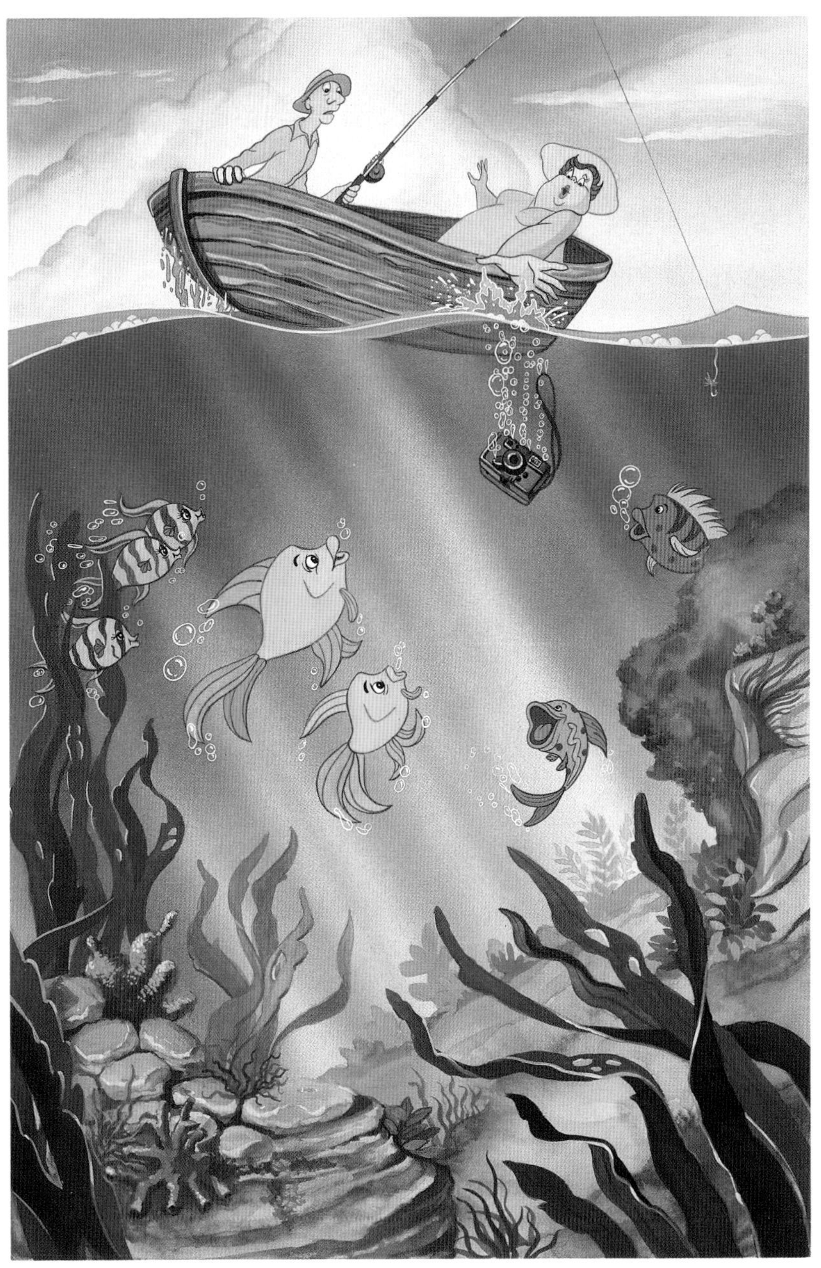

R O B B I N · C U D D Y

S.I. International · (212) 254-4996 · Fax (212) 995-0911
RSVP Callback Answering Service (718) 857-9267

TROPICAL

CHRiS REED

CHRIS REED • ILLUSTRATION
17 EDGEWOOD ROAD, EDISON, NJ 08820
908•548•3927 FAX: 908•603•0842

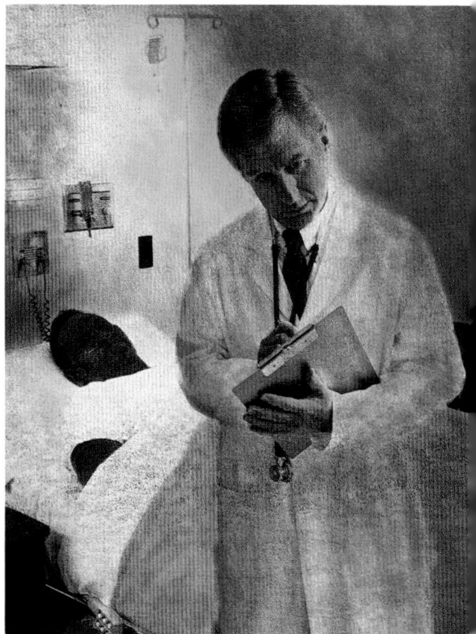

Joe Baker

PHOTO–MONTAGE PHOTOGRAPHY, 35 WOOSTER ST./SOHO, N.Y., N.Y. 10013
OIL AND COLORED PENCIL ON BLACK AND WHITE PHOTOGRAPHS
(212) 925–6555

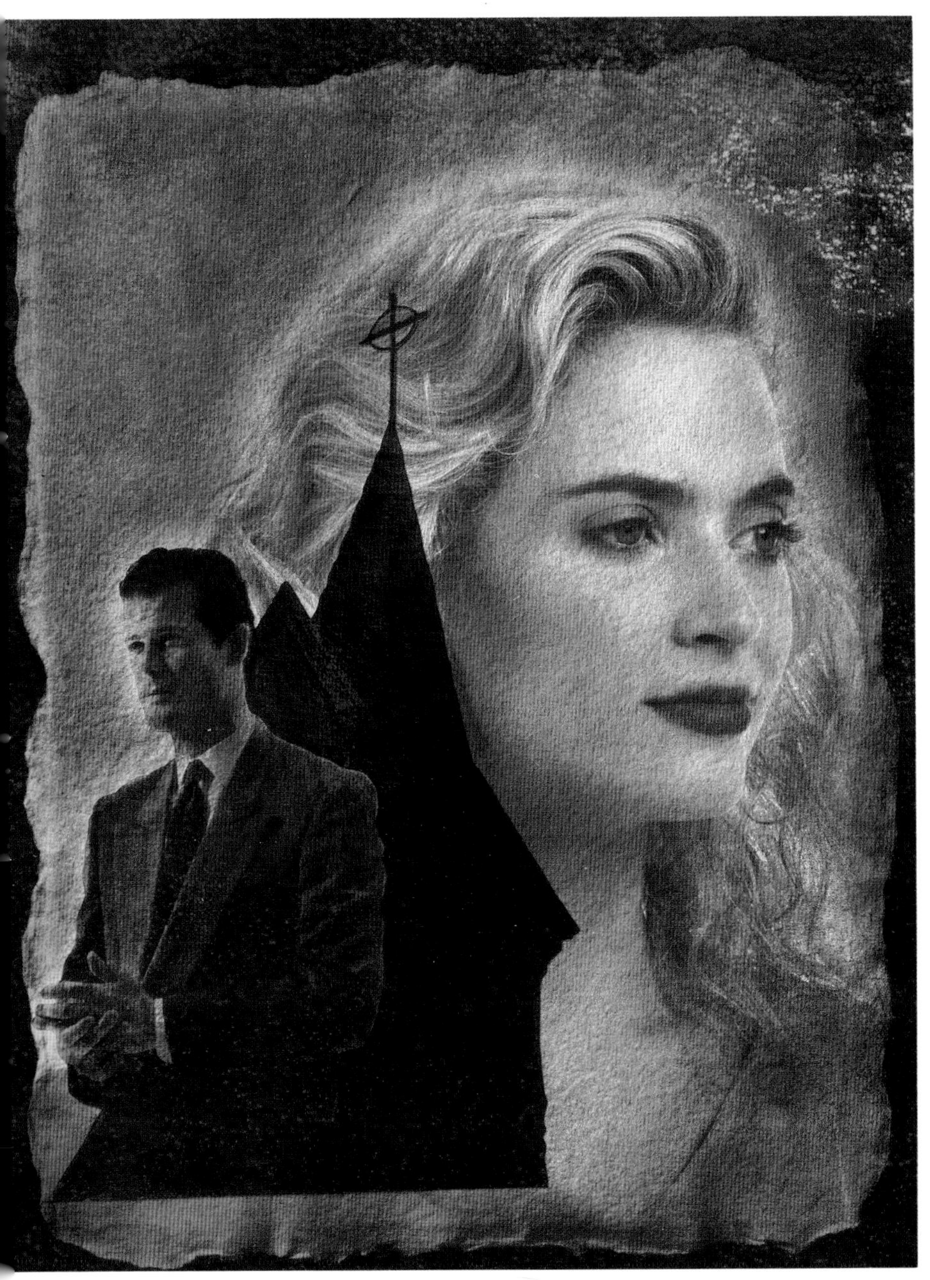

Joe Baker

PHOTO–MONTAGE PHOTOGRAPHY, 35 WOOSTER ST./SOHO, N.Y., N.Y. 10013
OIL AND COLORED PENCIL ON BLACK AND WHITE PHOTOGRAPHS
(212) 925–6555

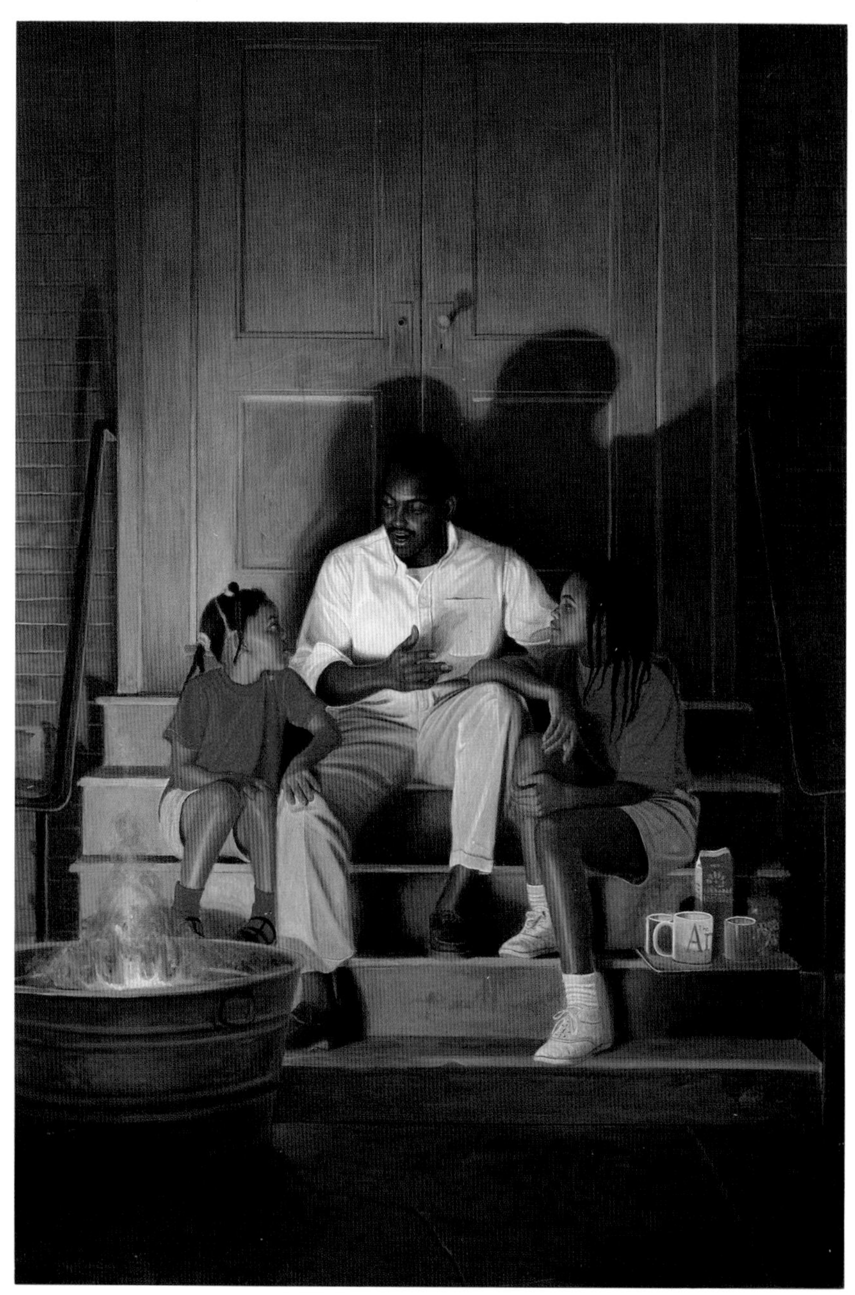

ERIC VELASQUEZ

ILLUSTRATOR
169 MANHATTAN AVE., NEW YORK, N.Y. 10025 (212) 316-3657
RSVP CALLBACK ANSWERING SERVICE (718) 857-9267

455 ORANGE, WYANDOTTE, MI 48192
(313) 283-4324

Roberto Parada

142 CANTERBURY AVE., N. ARLINGTON, N.J. 07031
(201) 998–0922

PAUL YALOWITZ
RSVP CALLBACK ANSWERING SERVICE (718) 857-9267

JANNINE MUELCHI

2925 VIA EMERADO, CARLSBAD, CA 92009
(619) 943-1196 FAX (619) 943-7412

TUKO FUJISAKI
(619) 494–5544, FAX IN STUDIO
CALL FOR MORE SAMPLES

Ron Bucalo

96 ALTAMONT AVE., TARRYTOWN, NY 10591 (914) 332-0174

JEANNE BERG, 250 SYLVAN RD., N. BABYLON, NY 11703 (516) 669-2366
CLIENTS: COSMOPOLITAN, ENTERTAINMENT WEEKLY, KNOPF,
L.A. TIMES, SCHOLASTIC, WASHINGTON POST

KENNETH FELD
RINGLING BROS AND BARNUM & BAILEY
THE GREATEST SHOW ON EARTH
CIRCUS
Bill Silvers
718-857-9267
216-899-1906

LORETTA GOMEZ

HUMOROUS ILLUSTRATION FROM HOBOKEN
201•656•5329 FAX 201•656•5329
RSVP CALLBACK ANSWERING SERVICE (718) 857-9267

PAUL VAN MUNCHING • ILLUSTRATION

RSVP CALL BACK ANSWERING SERVICE: 718•857•9267

Contact Harriet Kasak, 666 Greenwich Street, New York, NY 10014
Telephone (212) 675-5719, Fax (212) 675-6341

D A V I D W E N Z E L

Contact Harriet Kasak, 666 Greenwich Street, New York, NY 10014
Telephone (212) 675-5719, Fax (212) 675-6341

J A N P A L M E R

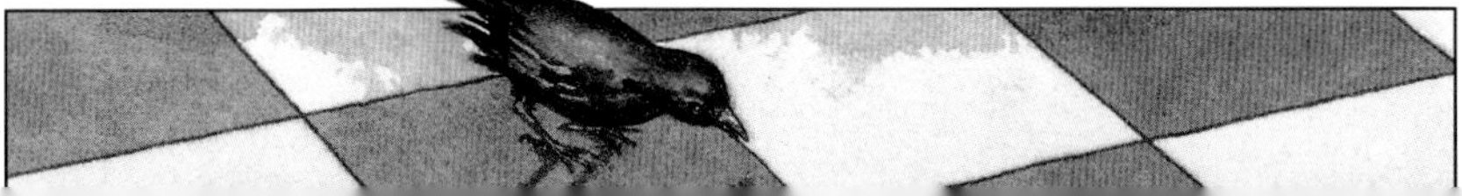

Contact Harriet Kasak, 666 Greenwich Street, New York, NY 10014
Telephone (212) 675-5719, Fax (212) 675-6341

P A U L M E I S E L

Contact Harriet Kasak, 666 Greenwich Street, New York, NY 10014
Telephone (212) 675-5719, Fax (212) 675-6341

KATHY EMBER

Contact Harriet Kasak, 666 Greenwich Street, New York, NY 10014
Telephone (212) 675-5719, Fax (212) 675-6341

Alice in Wonderland

The Ugly Bug Ball

Not Much of a Dog

Ferdinand

A N N E   K E N N E D Y

Contact Harriet Kasak, 666 Greenwich Street, New York, NY 10014
Telephone (212) 675-5719, Fax (212) 675-6341

RANDY VEROUGSTRAETE

Contact Harriet Kasak, 666 Greenwich Street, New York, NY 10014
Telephone (212) 675-5719, Fax (212) 675-6341

P E G G Y T A G E L

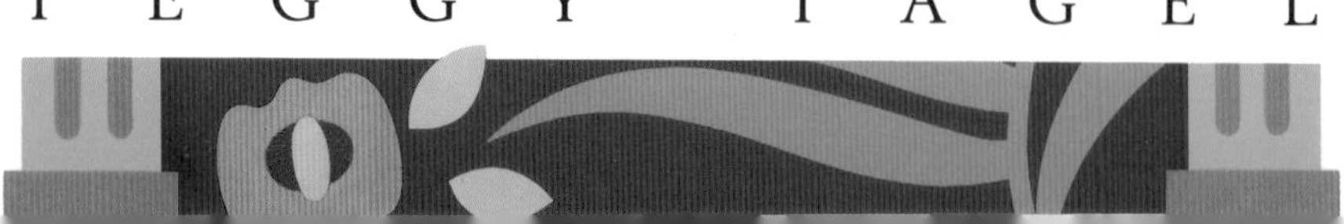

Contact Harriet Kasak, 666 Greenwich Street, New York, NY 10014
Telephone (212) 675-5719, Fax (212) 675-6341

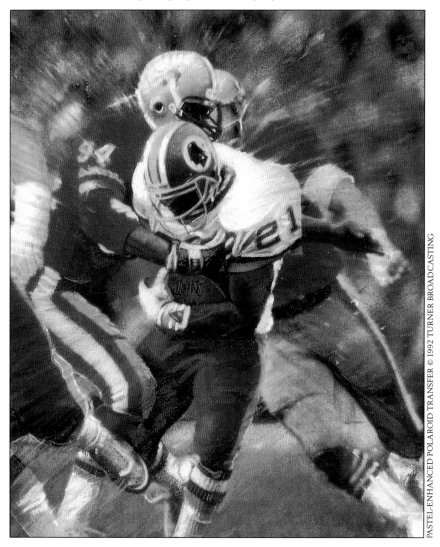

PASTEL-ENHANCED POLAROID TRANSFER © 1992 TURNER BROADCASTING

RICHARD ERICKSON

Contact Harriet Kasak, 666 Greenwich Street, New York, NY 10014
Telephone (212) 675-5719, Fax (212) 675-6341

S U S A N K E E T E R

Contact Harriet Kasak, 666 Greenwich Street, New York, NY 10014
Telephone (212) 675-5719, Fax (212) 675-6341

A L B E R T L E M A N T

NISHAN AKGULIAN
42–29 64TH STREET, WOODSIDE, NY 11377
(718) 565–6936

KLEMENTZ-HARTE

LAUREN KLEMENTZ–HARTE
203–235–6145/PO BOX 4006, MERIDEN, CT 06450
SEE ADDITIONAL WORK IN RSVP17

V.G. MYERS, 41 DOUGLAS RD., GLEN RIDGE, NJ 07028
201•429•8131 PHONE & FAX • ADDITIONAL WORK RSVP 13 & 15, AMERICAN SHOWCASE 13

L O R E T T A   L U S T I G

330 CLINTON AVENUE, BROOKLYN, N.Y. 11205 (718) 789–2496

JOSIE YEE
ILLUSTRATOR

211 W 20TH STREET
SUITE 6E
NEW YORK, NY
10011

Telephone
(212) 206-1260

Fax
(212) 627-6674

R.S.V.P. 16
R.S.V.P. 17

BRUCE WALDMAN

(718) 846–6411 • 83–44 LEFFERTS BLVD, #5B, KEW GARDENS, N.Y. 11415
RSVP CALLBACK ANSWERING SERVICE (718) 857-9267

deb hoeffner

538 CHERRY TREE LANE, KINNELON, NJ 07405
201–838–5490

ANNA VELTFORT
16 WEST 86 STREET, #B, NEW YORK, NY 10024
(212) 877-0430

GEORGE THOMPSON

34–50 28TH STREET • APT. 5B • ASTORIA, NY 11106
PHONE AND FAX (718) 937–2388
RSVP CALLBACK ANSWERING SERVICE (718) 857–9267

BARBARA GARRISON

ANOTHER CELEBRATED DANCING BEAR, CHARLES SCRIBNER'S NEW YORK TIMES
YEARS BEST ILLUSTRATED BOOKS

12 EAST 87TH STREET, NEW YORK, N.Y. 10128
(212) 348-6382, RSVP CALLBACK ANSWERING SERVICE (718) 857-9267

DEBORAH DUTKO
286 MOHEGAN ROAD, HUNTINGTON, CONNECTICUT 06430
203 • 925 • 0878

• Nancy Didion •

33 MOOSE HILL PARKWAY, SHARON, MA 02067
(617) 784-1389 FAX (617) 784-1391

JOHNNY
1962-1992
KENT GAMBLE

ILLUSTRATION

192 17TH ST, BROOKLYN, NY 11215 (718) 768-3296
FAX IN STUDIO. ALSO SEE AMERICAN SHOWCASE 15 & 16

hammer
time
boom
boom
BOOM
boom
NINETEEN NINETY T.W.O
MARK T. SMITH
boom
BOOM
boom
BOOM
MARK T. SMITH ©1992.
(212) 673 8446.

KARL DENHAM

ILLUSTRATOR
PHONE: 201-792-6422 FAX: 201-792-0658

FISHING FOR FUNNY BUSINESS
TOM HUFFMAN (212) 819–0211
FAX AVAILABLE

TOMMASO GIANNOTTA

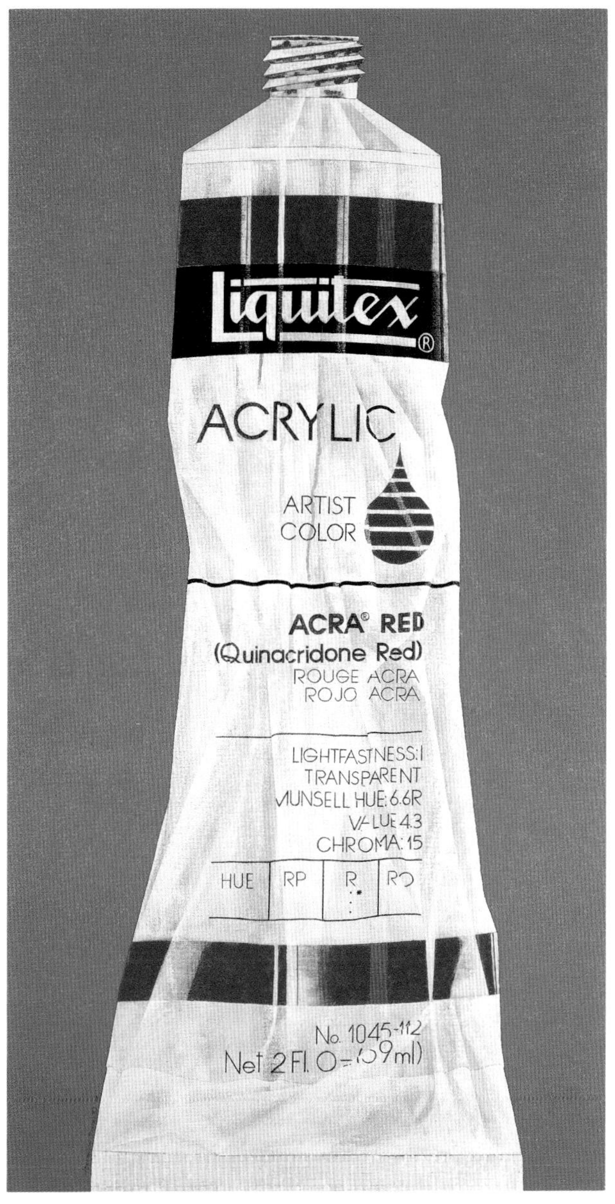

FLEETWOOD FINE ARTS

304 HUDSON STREET NYC 10013 212 924 4422

T E R R A N C E

210 WEST 64 STREET # 5B NEW YORK, NY 10023 PHONE / FAX 212-586-419

C U M M I N G S

210 WEST 64 STREET # 5B NEW YORK, NY 10023 PHONE / FAX 212 586-4193

EVAN POLENGHI
ILLUSTRATION
159-25TH STREET
BKLYN, N.Y. 11232
718 • 499 • 3214
REPRESENTED BY
JEAN CONLON
212 • 966 • 9897
Clients Include:
American Express
New York Times
Time Inc.
Sports Illustrated for Kids
Pratt Institute, Art and Design
Sacks & Rosen Advertising
Joseph and Feiss Company
Carillon Importers,
Absolut Vodka
MacMillan Publishing
Harcourt Brace Jovanovich
Fairchild Publications
Metropolitan Life
NYC Transit Authority
International Thomson
Retail Press
Institute for Electronic and
Electrical Engineers
Fratelli Rossetti NYC
Ms Magazine

LAINÉ ROUNDY

42 BUTTONBALL DRIVE, SANDY HOOK, CT 06482
PHONE (203) 426-9531 FAX (203) 270-7223

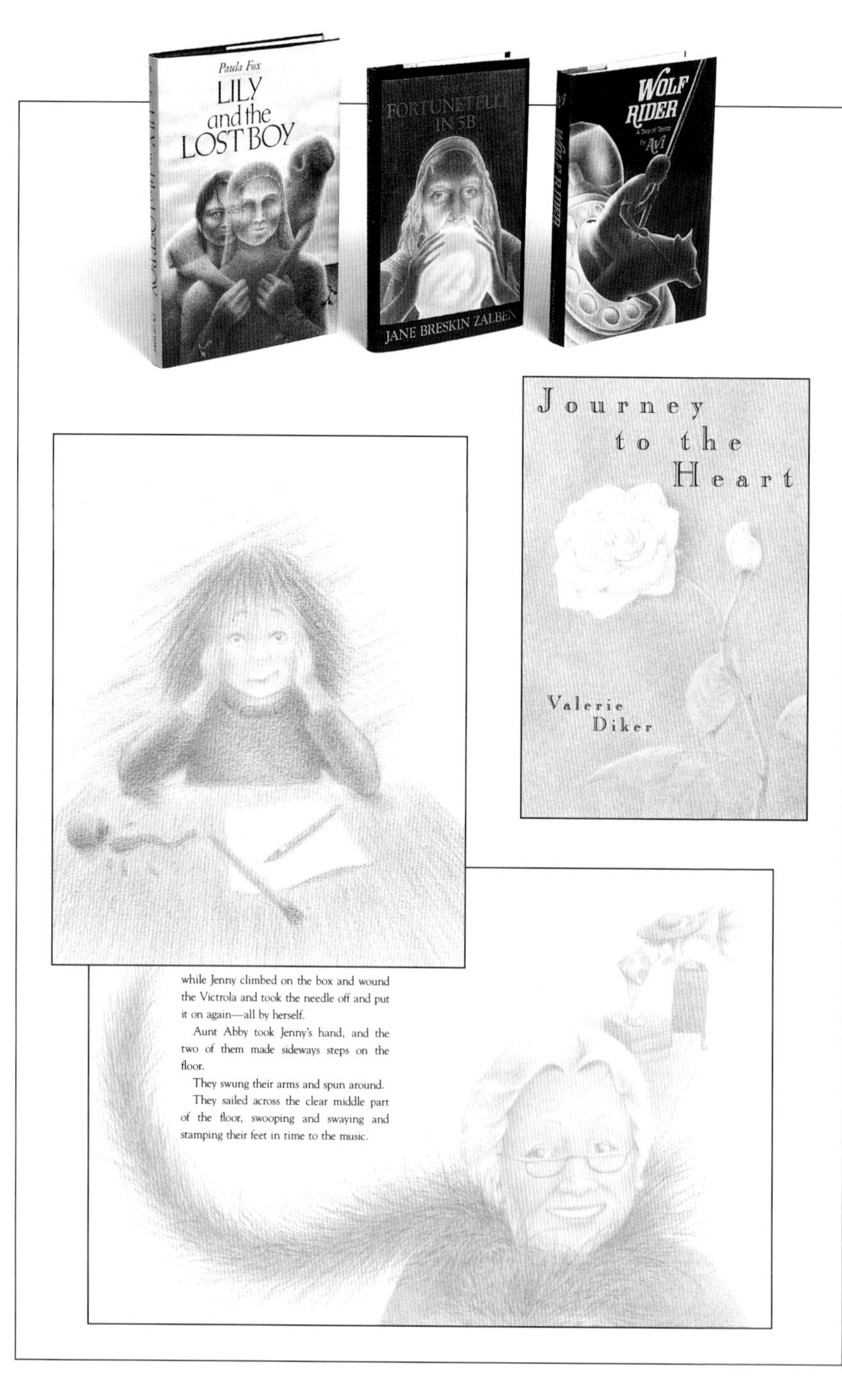

Paula Fox
LILY and the LOST BOY
FORTUNETELLER IN 5B
JANE BRESKIN ZALBEN
WOLF RIDER
A Tale of Terror
by Avi
Journey to the Heart
Valerie Diker
while Jenny climbed on the box and wound the Victrola and took the needle off and put it on again—all by herself.
Aunt Abby took Jenny's hand, and the two of them made sideways steps on the floor.
They swung their arms and spun around.
They sailed across the clear middle part of the floor, swooping and swaying and stamping their feet in time to the music.

BARBARA J. ROMAN
212•362•1374
SPECIALIZING IN ADVERTISING, PACKAGING & PUBLISHING ILLUSTRATION

George Schmidt

183 STEUBEN STREET, BROOKLYN, N.Y. 11205 (718) 857-1837

ROSE MARY BERLIN OF BERLIN PRODUCTIONS
LOCKE LANE RD#1 BOX 193 • YORKTOWN HTS., NY 10598
(914) 962–0526 • FAX (914) 962–2266

NINA LADEN ILLUSTRATES
1517 MCLENDON AVE. N.E., • ATLANTA, • GA • 30307
(404) 371-0052 • (800) 743-5196

EMILY THOMPSON

34–50 28TH STREET • APT. 5B • ASTORIA, NY 11106
PHONE AND FAX (718) 937–2388
RSVP CALLBACK ANSWERING SERVICE (718) 857–9267

JOE GYURCSAK

REPRESENTED BY • LISA GYURCSAK

133 EATON AVENUE • MERCERVILLE, NJ 08619 • 609-586-7007

(718) 625–1264 MEAN PICTURES DRAWN FOR MCGRAW–HILL,
GOOD HOUSEKEEPING, MEDICAL ECONOMICS, VIKING PENGUIN BOOKS, VOGUE
RSVP CALLBACK ANSWERING SERVICE (718) 857–9267

ANIMATICS
POW!
ANIMATION
DESIGN
COMIC BOOK
STUFF.

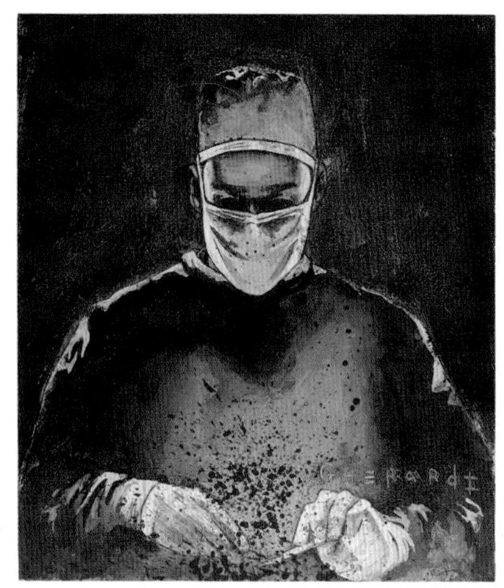

bob Gherardi

78 HAMPSHIRE DRIVE, PLAINSBORO, N.J. 08536
(609) 936-9138

DONNA A. CORVI ILLUSTRATION/DINKO INK, INC.
1591 SECOND AVENUE, NEW YORK, N.Y. 10028
(212) 628•3102

Kevin Cuddy

190 HENR

STAMFORD, CT 06902, TELEPHONE (203) 325-9997, FAX (203) 359-6973

Manuel King

SHERYL BERANBAUM ARTISTS' REPRESENTATIVE
TEL 617•437•9459 TEL 401•737•8591 FAX 617•437•6494

Stephen Moscowitz

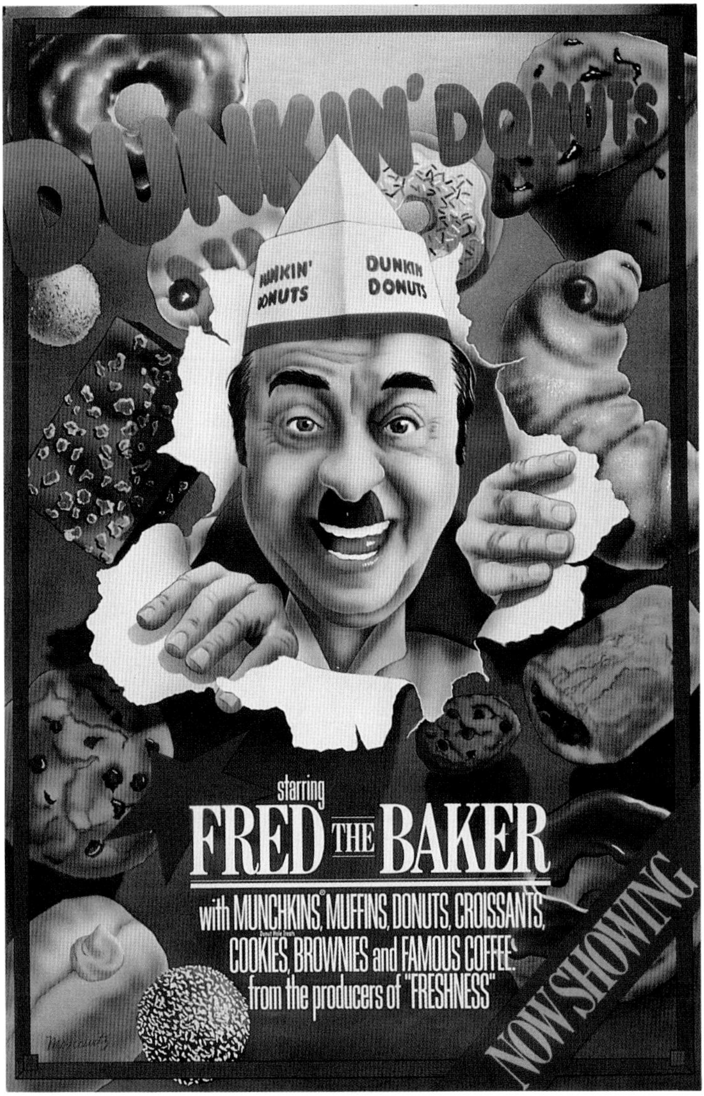

SHERYL BERANBAUM ARTISTS' REPRESENTATIVE
TEL 617•437•9459 TEL 401•737•8591 FAX 617•437•6494

James Edwards

SHERYL BERANBAUM ARTISTS' REPRESENTATIVE
TEL 617•437•9459 TEL 401•737•8591 FAX 617•437•6494

Mike Gardner

SHERYL BERANBAUM ARTISTS' REPRESENTATIVE
TEL 617•437•9459 TEL 401•737•8591 FAX 617•437•6494

Lee Corey

SHERYL BERANBAUM ARTISTS' REPRESENTATIVE
TEL 617•437•9459 TEL 401•737•8591 FAX 617•437•6494

John Kastner

stARTling images

SHERYL BERANBAUM ARTISTS' REPRESENTATIVE
TEL 617•437•9459 TEL 401•737•8591 FAX 617•437•6494

Lane Gregory

GWEN WALTERS GOLDSTEIN

50 Fuller Brook Road • Wellesley, MA 02181

6 1 7 • 2 3 5 • 8 6 5 8

Larry Johnson

GWEN WALTERS GOLDSTEIN

50 Fuller Brook Road • Wellesley, MA 02181

6 1 7 • 2 3 5 • 8 6 5 8

Dan Krovatin

GWEN WALTERS GOLDSTEIN
50 Fuller Brook Road • Wellesley, MA 02181
6 1 7 • 2 3 5 • 8 6 5 8

Kathleen O'Malley

GWEN WALTERS GOLDSTEIN
50 Fuller Brook Road • Wellesley, MA 02181
6 1 7 • 2 3 5 • 8 6 5 8

Pat Soper

GWEN WALTERS GOLDSTEIN

50 Fuller Brook Road • Wellesley, MA 02181

6 1 7 • 2 3 5 • 8 6 5 8

Gary Phillips

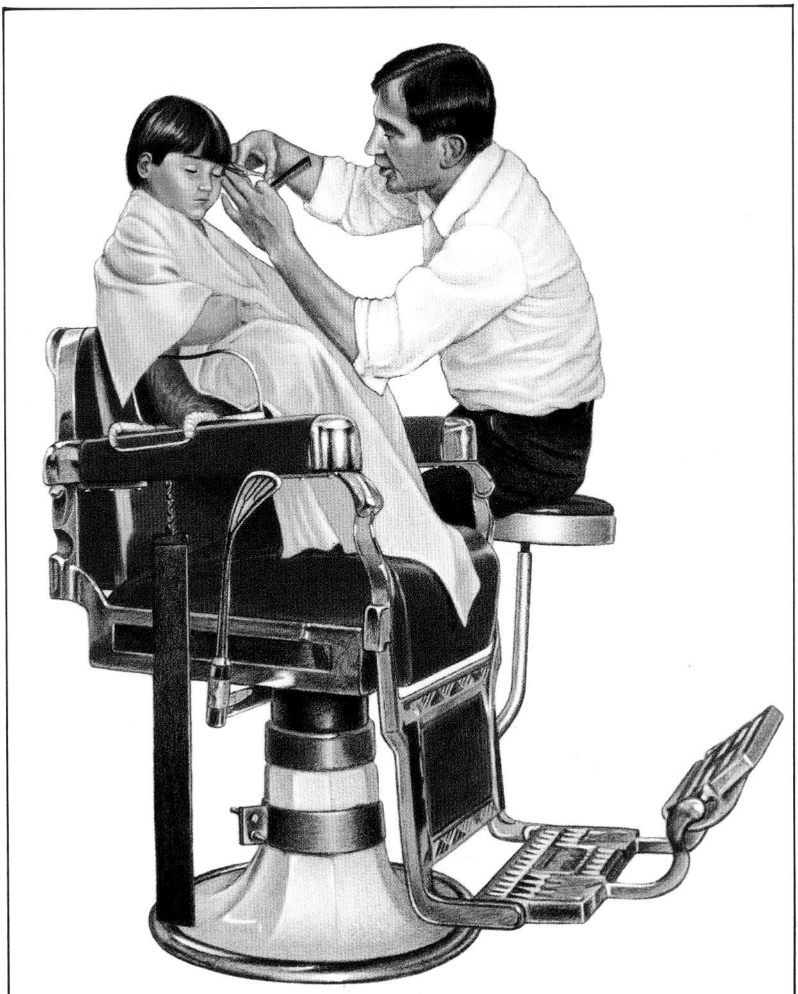

GWEN WALTERS GOLDSTEIN

50 Fuller Brook Road • Wellesley, MA 02181

6 1 7 • 2 3 5 • 8 6 5 8

Susan Spellman

GWEN WALTERS GOLDSTEIN
50 Fuller Brook Road • Wellesley, MA 02181
6 1 7 • 2 3 5 • 8 6 5 8

Gary Torrisi

MARTIN LUTHER
KING, JR.
January 15, 1929 - April 4, 1968

The New York Times
MARTIN LUTHER KING ACCEPTS THE NOBEL PEACE PRIZE IN OSLO, NORWAY.

A Salute to Black History

We proudly salute the legacy of black achievement. The men and women who pioneered black advancement did so with limited resources. They truly are positive role models. Their determination and skills have enriched our country with great scholars, civil rights advocates, entertainers, journalists, entrepreneurs, scientists, educators, athletes, military and government officials – and on!

Hardee's

WWIN 1400 95.9

GWEN WALTERS GOLDSTEIN
50 Fuller Brook Road • Wellesley, MA 02181
6 1 7 • 2 3 5 • 8 6 5 8

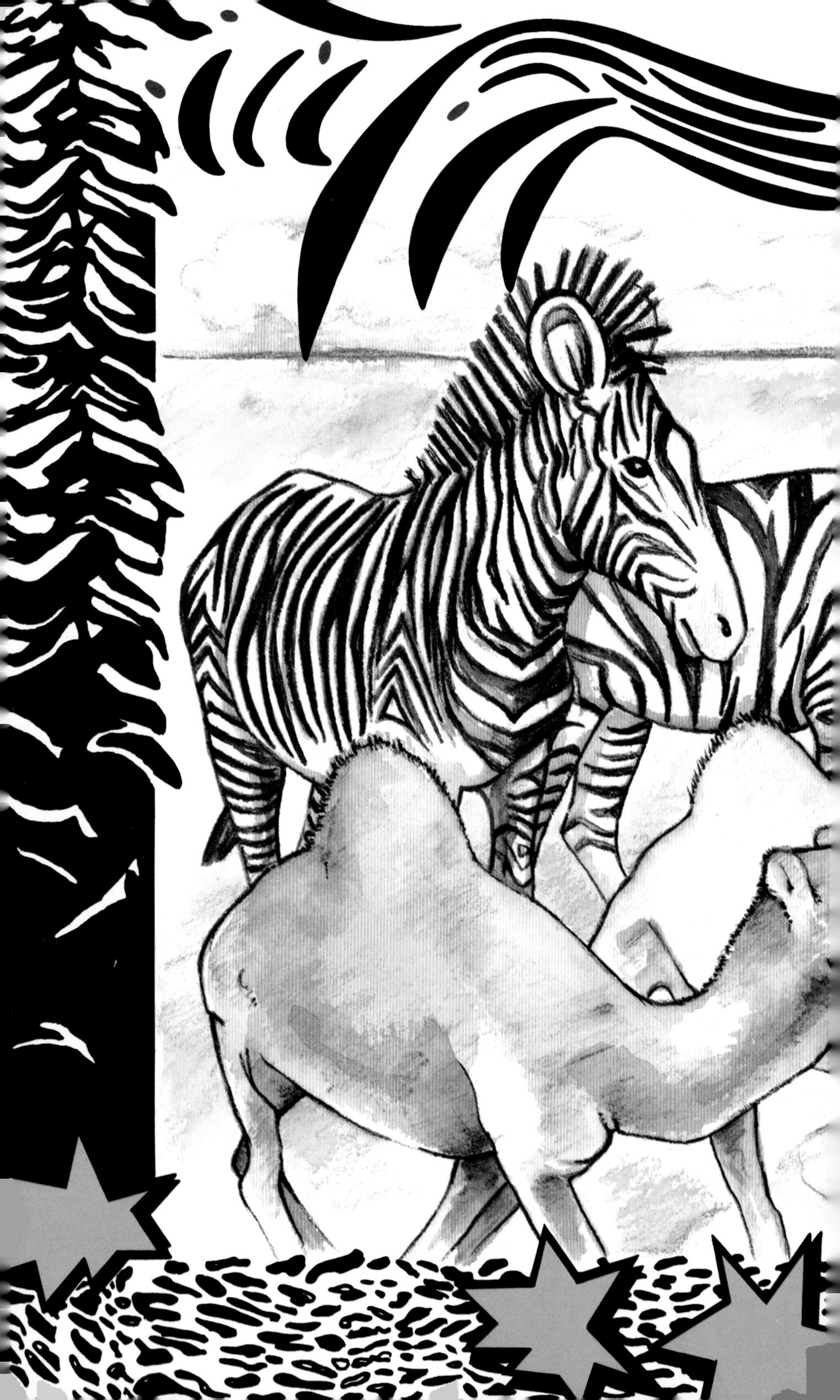

Emma
Crawford
GRAPHIC
ILLUSTRATION
and DESIGN
108 East 16th Street
New York, NY 10003
Tel: 212 • 420 • 1222
Fax: 212 • 673 • 5236

Rick Stromoski

Humorous Illustration

(203) 668-8738

Fax (203) 668-8742

CLIENTS INCLUDE: CBS TELEVISION, RECYCLED PAPER PRODUCTS, TRISAR, PLAYBOY, ESQUIRE, OMNI, INFORMATIONWEEK, WEEKLY READER CORP., UNIVERSAL PRESS SYNDICATE

TINY TOWN PRESS
BOOKS
BOOKS
BOOKS
TINY TOWN PRESS
COOKING FOR BUCKS
TRAVEL
MYSTERY
SURVIVAL TACTICS

Ray Cruz

Co-Represented by

For Publishing

9 Babbling Brook Lane, Suffern, New York 10901
(914) 368-8606

For Corporate & Advertising

Jane Chambless Wright

9 Babbling Brook Lane, Suffern, New York 10901

Robert Frank

REPRESENTED BY 

(914) 368-8606

9 Babbling Brook Lane, Suffern, New York 10901

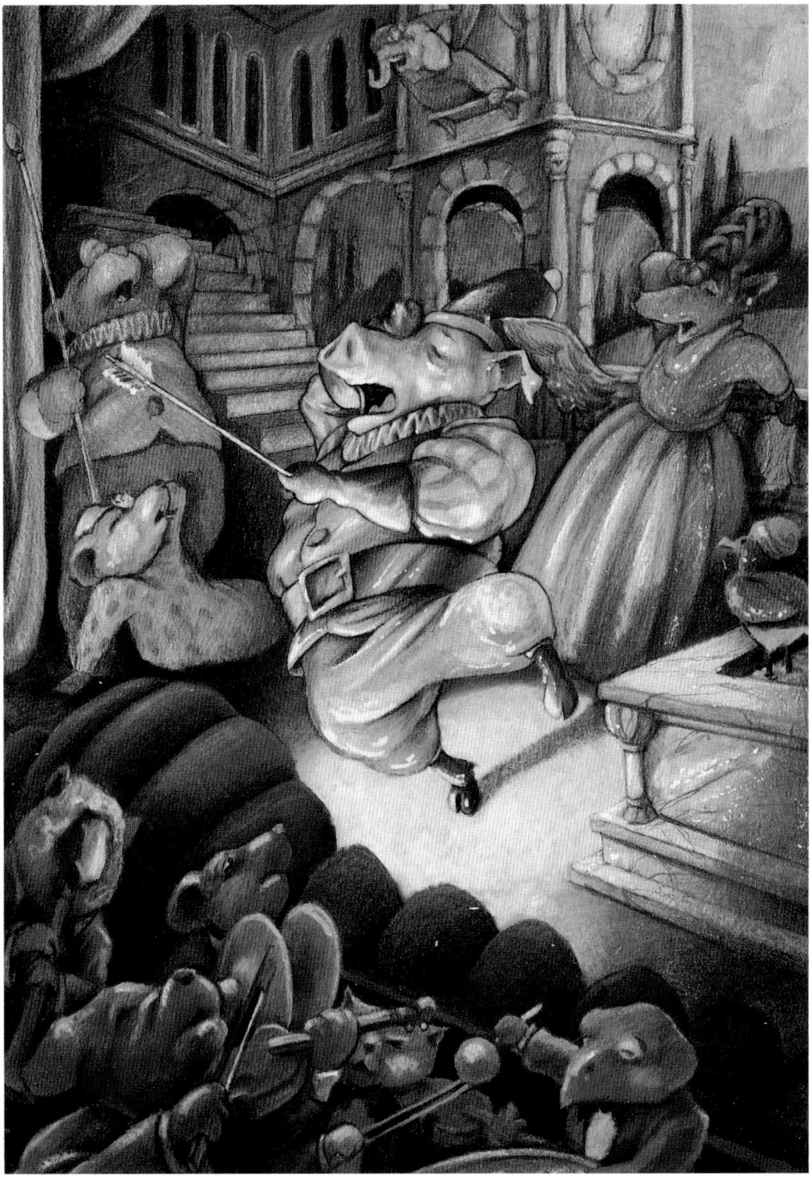

Kevin O'Malley

9 Babbling Brook Lane, Suffern, New York 10901

CHRIS ALLAN
3240 HENRY HUDSON PKWY #6F, BRONX, N.Y. 10463
PHONE/FAX: (718) 601-3743, RSVP CALLBACK SERVICE (718) 857-9267

AARON KOSTER
2 YEOMAN WAY, MANALAPAN, NJ 07726
(908) 536–2815

Elizabeth Williams
212-945-6442
Reportage art & illustration
clients include:
Ammirati & Puris,
Newsday, The New York Times,
Scholastic, Houghton Mifflin,
CBS, NBC, ABC-TV,
Islands Mag.

Bob Mackie #87
'91 Fall Collection Show

Diversions Mag.

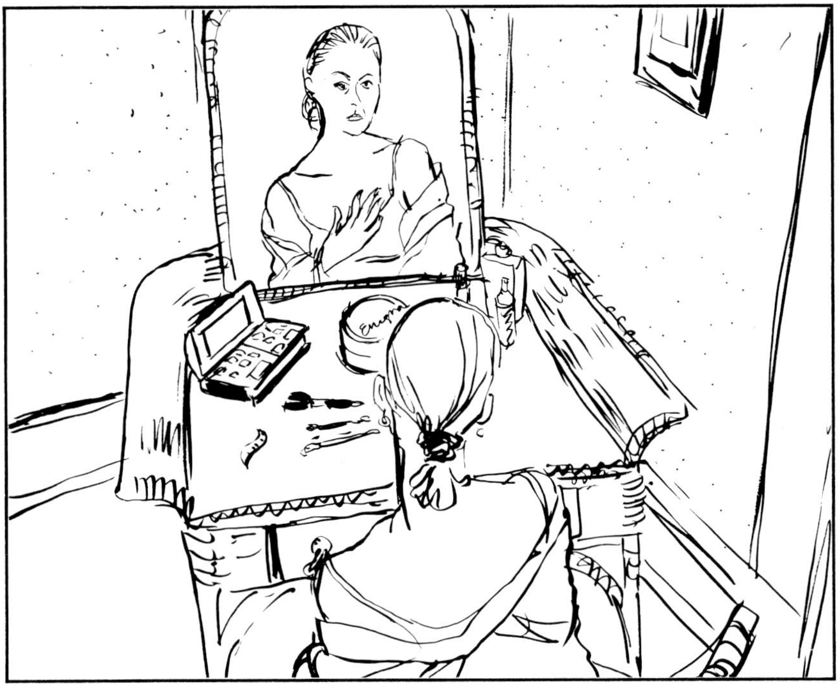

Healthstate Mag.

WCBS News

KARL FISCHER: CARTOON & ANIMATION SPECIALIST • TELEPHONE: 914–737–5690
ADDRESS: 9 PINE HILL ROAD • CROTON, NEW YORK 10520
CLIENTS: CBS–TV • PEPSICO • YOUNG & RUBICAM • TIME/WARNER • CTW

(212) 795–4941, 875 WEST 181 ST., NYC 10033
RSVP CALLBACK ANSWERING SERVICE (718) 857–9267

CECILY LANG

336 WEST END AVENUE, NEW YORK, NY 10023 TEL: (212) 580-3424.
RSVP CALLBACK ANSWERING SERVICE (718) 857-9267. ADDITIONAL WORK MAY BE SEEN IN 3 DIMENSIONAL AWARDS ANNUAL. FAX AVAILABLE.

Lane Yerkes ***Represented by Philip M. Veloric***

PHILIP M. VELORIC • ARTIST'S REPRESENTATIVE
128 BEECHTREE DRIVE; BROOMALL, PA 19008
PHONE: (215) 356•0362 • FAX: (215) 353•7531

Len Ebert *Represented by Philip M. Veloric*

PHILIP M. VELORIC • ARTIST'S REPRESENTATIVE
128 BEECHTREE DRIVE, BROOMALL, PA 19008
PHONE: (215) 356•0362 • FAX: (215) 353•7531

Don Dyen *Represented by Philip M. Veloric*

PHILIP M. VELORIC • ARTIST'S REPRESENTATIVE
128 BEECHTREE DRIVE, BROOMALL, PA 19008
PHONE: (215) 356 • 0362 • FAX: (215) 353 • 7531

Rebecca A. Merrilees *Represented by Philip M. Veloric*

PHILIP M. VELORIC • ARTIST'S REPRESENTATIVE
128 BEECHTREE DRIVE, BROOMALL, PA 19008
PHONE: (215) 356•0362 • FAX: (215) 353•7531

Deb Bunnell *Represented by Philip M. Veloric*

PHILIP M. VELORIC • ARTIST'S REPRESENTATIVE
128 BEECHTREE DRIVE; BROOMALL, PA 19008
PHONE: (215) 356 • 0362 • FAX: (215) 353 • 7531

John Holder *Represented by Philip M. Veloric*

PHILIP M. VELORIC • ARTIST'S REPRESENTATIVE
128 BEECHTREE DRIVE; BROOMALL, PA 19008
PHONE: (215) 356•0362 • FAX: (215) 353•7531

Rick Cooley *Represented by Philip M. Veloric*

PHILIP M. VELORIC • ARTIST'S REPRESENTATIVE
128 BEECHTREE DRIVE, BROOMALL, PA 19008
PHONE: (215) 356•0362 • FAX: (215) 353•7531

BRYNA WALDMAN
REPRESENTATIVE LEE FISHBACK
ILLUSTRATIONS INC. (212) 929-2951/(201) 568-4868

© SANDY SHIELDS WATERCOLOR PONIES PUBLISHED BY WORD INC.

REPRESENTED BY (203) 438-8386

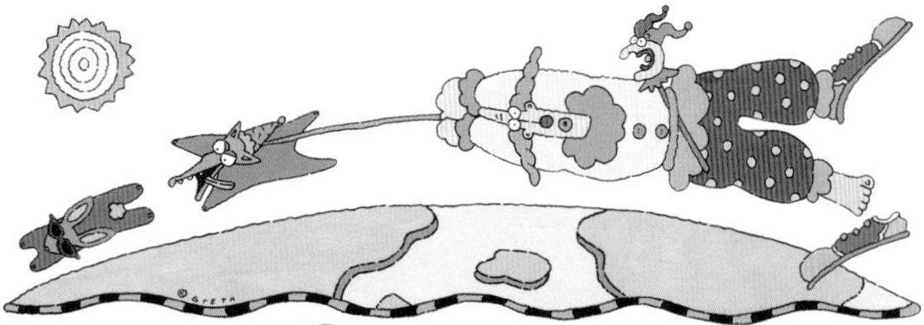

Greta Buchart

REPRESENTED BY

(203) 438-8386

© JOEL ISKOWITZ WHY I LEFT HARRY'S ALL NIGHT HAMBURGERS PUBLISHED BY DELACORTE PRESS

Joel Iskowitz

REPRESENTED BY 

(203) 438-8386

REPRESENTED BY

(203) 438-8386

© NANCY MANTHA

nancy mantha

© ANN IOSA

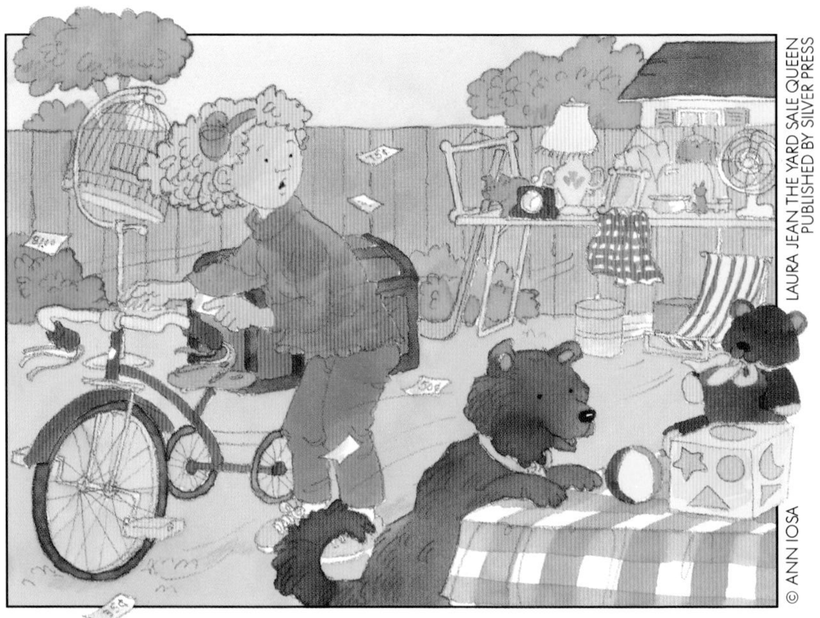

LAURA JEAN THE YARD SALE QUEEN
PUBLISHED BY SILVER PRESS

© ANN IOSA

Ann W. Iosa

REPRESENTED BY

(203) 438-8386

maggie staton

REPRESENTED BY

(203) 438-8386

REPRESENTED BY

(203) 438-8386

© LINDA GRAVES THE LITTLE RED HEN
PUBLISHED BY MCDOUGAL LITTEL

© LINDA GRAVES THE WISE WOMEN AND HER SECRET
PUBLISHED BY SIMON & SCHUSTER

Linda Graves

REPRESENTED BY 

(203) 438-8386

C. Shana Greger

REPRESENTED BY

(203) 438-8386

© CHI CHUNG THE TREASURE HUNT
PUBLISHED BY MODERN CURRICULUM PRESS

CHI CHUNG © GOLDILOCKS AND THE THREE BEARS
PUBLISHED BY WORLD BOOK

Chi Chung

REPRESENTED BY 

(203) 438-8386

RSVP
THE DIRECTORY OF ILLUSTRATION AND DESIGN
18
MATTELSON

DESIGN

Gold & Platinum Records

DAVID MYERS GRAPHICS
LETTERING & AIRBRUSH ILLUSTRATION
(212) 989-5260

WELL CRAFTED ART.

Award winning design and illustration of logos, posters, covers, packaging, displays & promotions. Conception through final art. I'll craft your project into something that makes us both proud. Your layout or mine...lets put our heads together.

BRIAN DUGAN 908·396·1231 phone & fax

N

HIGH
ADVENTURE
TALES

S

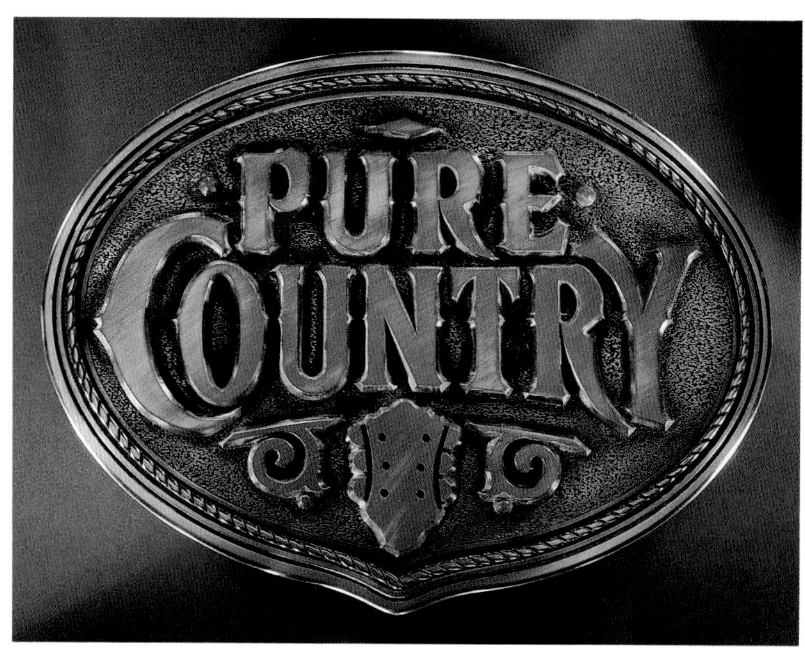

TOM NIKOSEY DESIGN
818/704.9993 FAX 818/704.9995

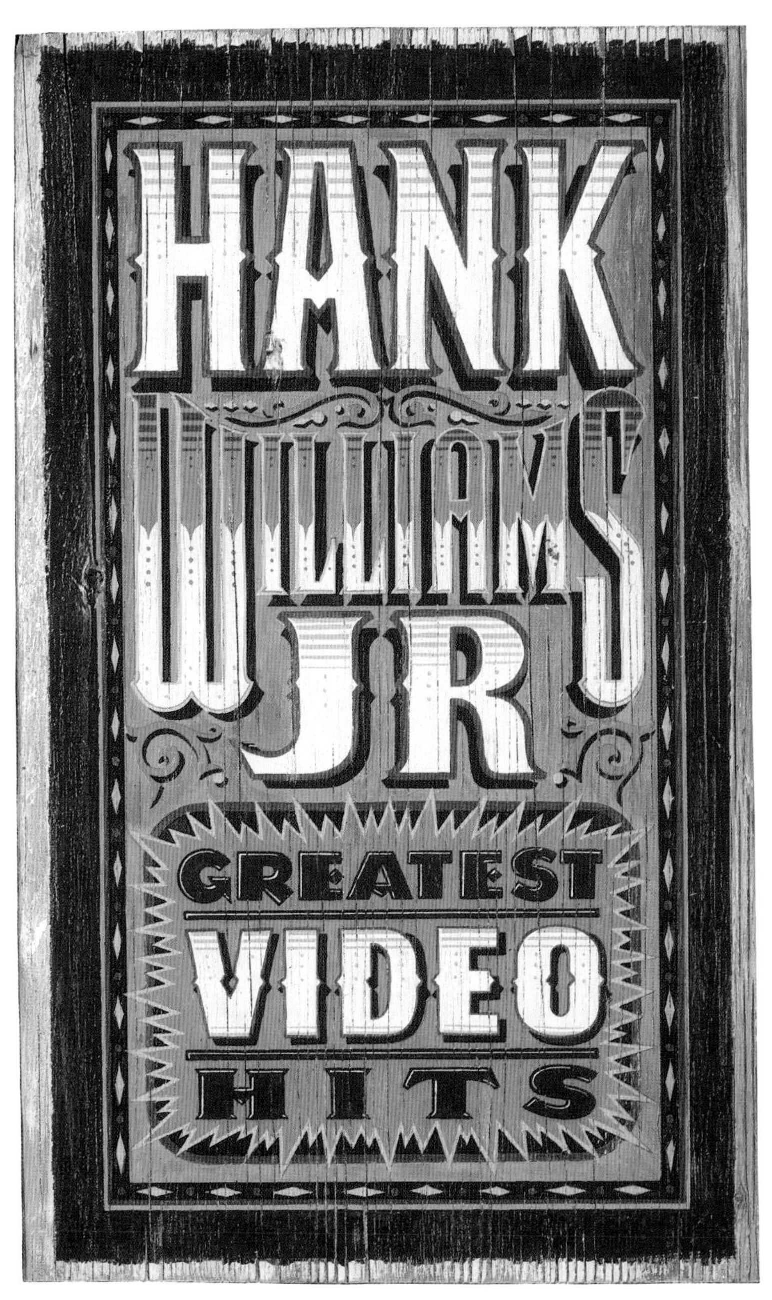
HANK
WILLIAMS
JR.
GREATEST
VIDEO
HITS

CAROLCO

Nielsen
Category
Management

X-PRESSIT

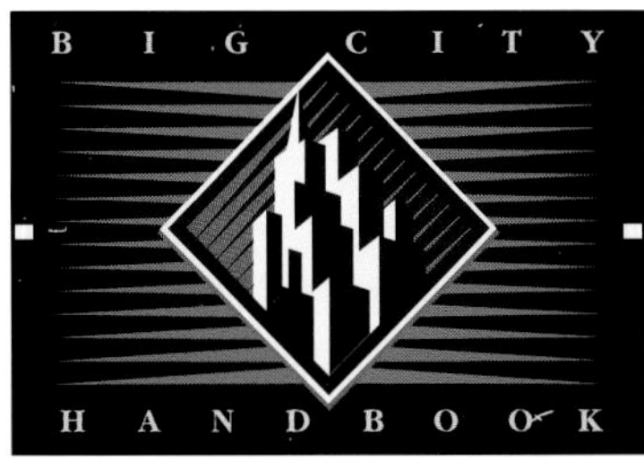
BIG CITY
HANDBOOK

ASK
ZANDAR

DEBEST
DESIGN
DESEALED
DELIVERED

AGAZINES • ADVERTISING • PROMOTION • DIRECT MAIL • PACKAGING

CHARD BLEIWEISS DESIGN
557 LEFFERTS PLACE
ELLMORE, NEW YORK 11710
HONE & FAX •516-679-9391

DE END.

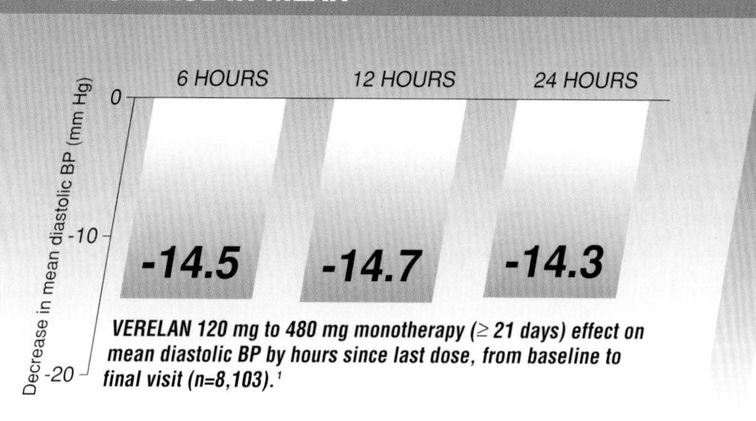

VERELAN 120 mg to 480 mg monotherapy (≥ 21 days) effect on mean diastolic BP by hours since last dose, from baseline to final visit (n=8,103).[1]

Downtown Richmond, Virginia

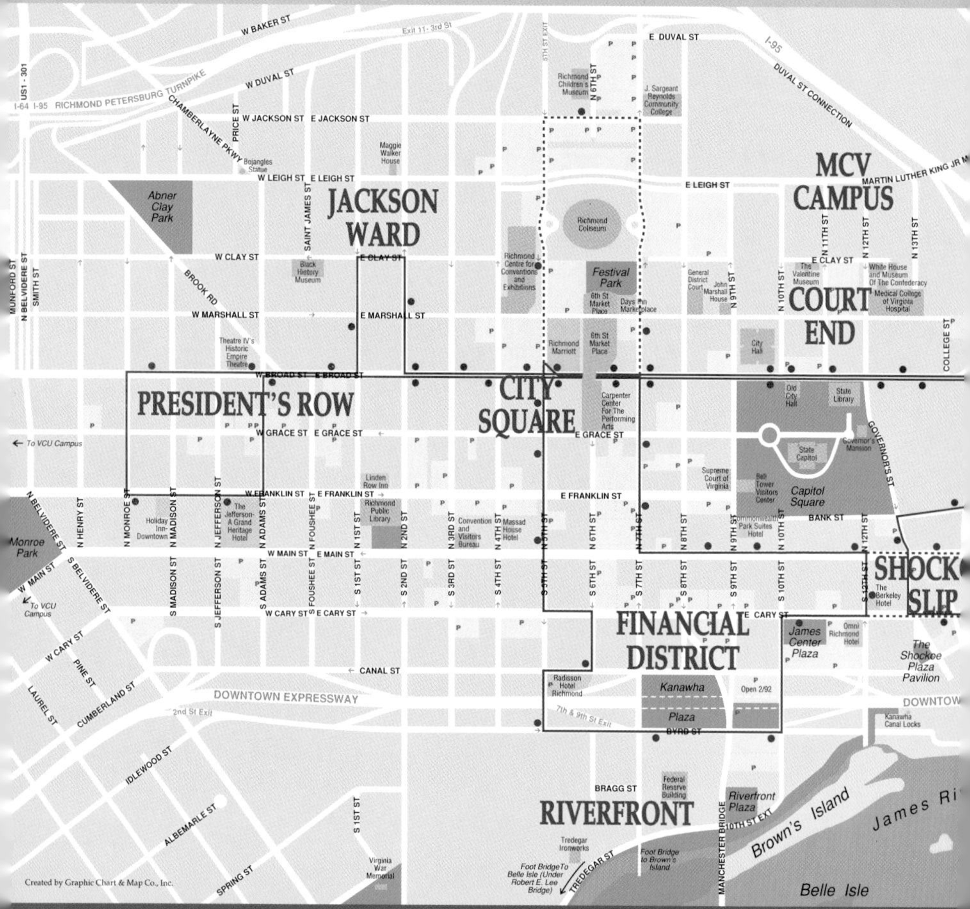

Created by Graphic Chart & Map Co., Inc.

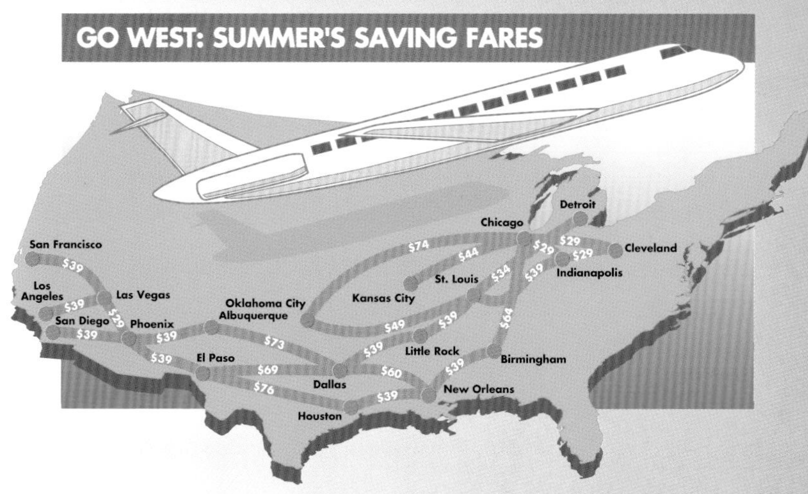
GO WEST: SUMMER'S SAVING FARES
San Francisco
Los Angeles
Las Vegas
San Diego
Phoenix
Oklahoma City
Albuquerque
El Paso
Dallas
Houston
Kansas City
St. Louis
Little Rock
Chicago
Detroit
Cleveland
Indianapolis
Birmingham
New Orleans
$39
$29
$73
$69
$76
$60
$74
$44
$34
$49
$64

O ST
Major Attractions, Landmarks
Hotels
Parks, Public Areas
Parking Lot Entrances
Trolley Routes
6th Street Marketplace-Riverfront Route
6th Street Marketplace-Riverfront Extended Route
Broad Street-Shockoe Slip Route
Trolley Stop
SCALE
feet 0 500 1000
Directional Signs for Downtown Parking
To St. John's Church
N 20TH ST
CRANE ST
E GRACE ST
AMBLER ST
N 17TH ST
N 18TH ST
N 19TH ST
E FRANKLIN ST
THE BOTTOM
Farmer's Market
E MAIN ST
Poe Museum
S 17TH ST
S 19TH ST
S 20TH ST
E CARY ST
DOCK ST
I-95 RICHMOND PETERSBURG TURNPIKE

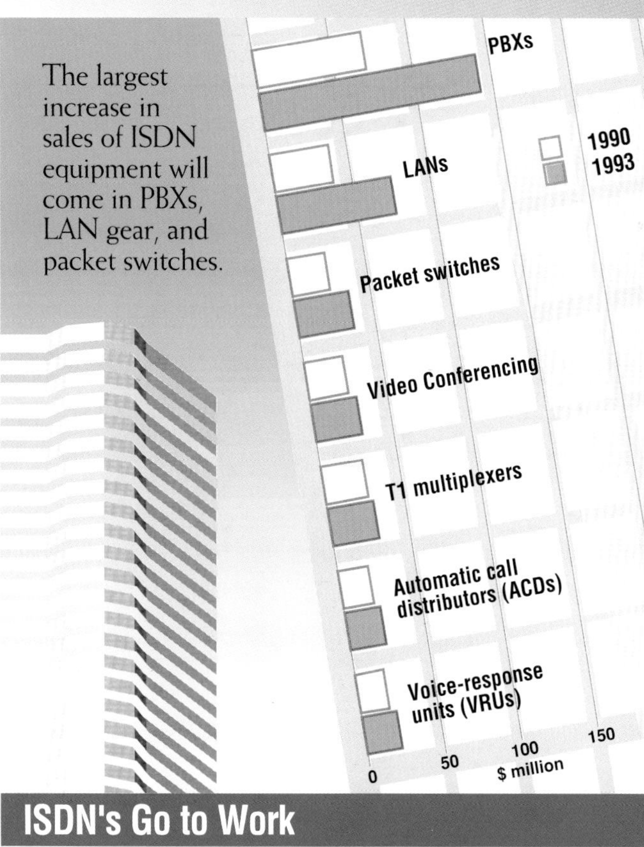
The largest increase in sales of ISDN equipment will come in PBXs, LAN gear, and packet switches.
PBXs
LANs
1990
1993
Packet switches
Video Conferencing
T1 multiplexers
Automatic call distributors (ACDs)
Voice-response units (VRUs)
0
50
100
150
$ million
ISDN's Go to Work

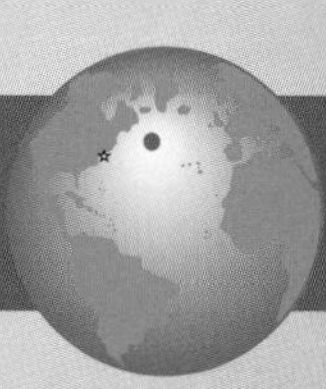

ILLUSTRATION

ANGELO

ARTIST/ILLUSTRATOR EXTRAORDINAIRE
1449 LONGFELLOW AVENUE, BRONX, NY 10459
(718) 617–2907, RSVP CALLBACK ANSWERING SERVICE (718) 857–9267

Richard Lebenson

253 WASHINGTON AVENUE, BROOKLYN, N.Y. 11205 (718) 857-9267

Richard Lebenson

253 WASHINGTON AVENUE, BROOKLYN, N.Y. 11205 (718) 857-9267

STEPHEN HARRINGTON

REPRESENTED BY JOHN BREWSTER CREATIVE SERVICES
597 RIVERSIDE AVENUE, WESTPORT, CT 06880
(203) 226-4724 FAX (203) 454-9904

STEPHEN HARRINGTON

REPRESENTED BY JOHN BREWSTER CREATIVE SERVICES
597 RIVERSIDE AVENUE, WESTPORT, CT 06880
(203) 226-4724 FAX (203) 454-9904

HOUSE PAYMENTS
J.C. JOHNSON
WordPerfect
for IBM Personal Computers
J.C. JOHNSON
JUDGE
J.C. JOHNSON

Darren Thompson

Illustrator

404 E. 38th Street

Anderson, IN 46013

Phone & Fax: 317-641-7046

FULL-COLOR WORK UPON REQUEST
RSVP CALLBACK ANSWERING SERVICE (718) 857-9267

DORIS ETTLINGER

RD 2 BOX 6, IMLAYDALE ROAD, HAMPTON, N.J. 08827
PHONE (908) 537–6322 FAX (908) 537–7966

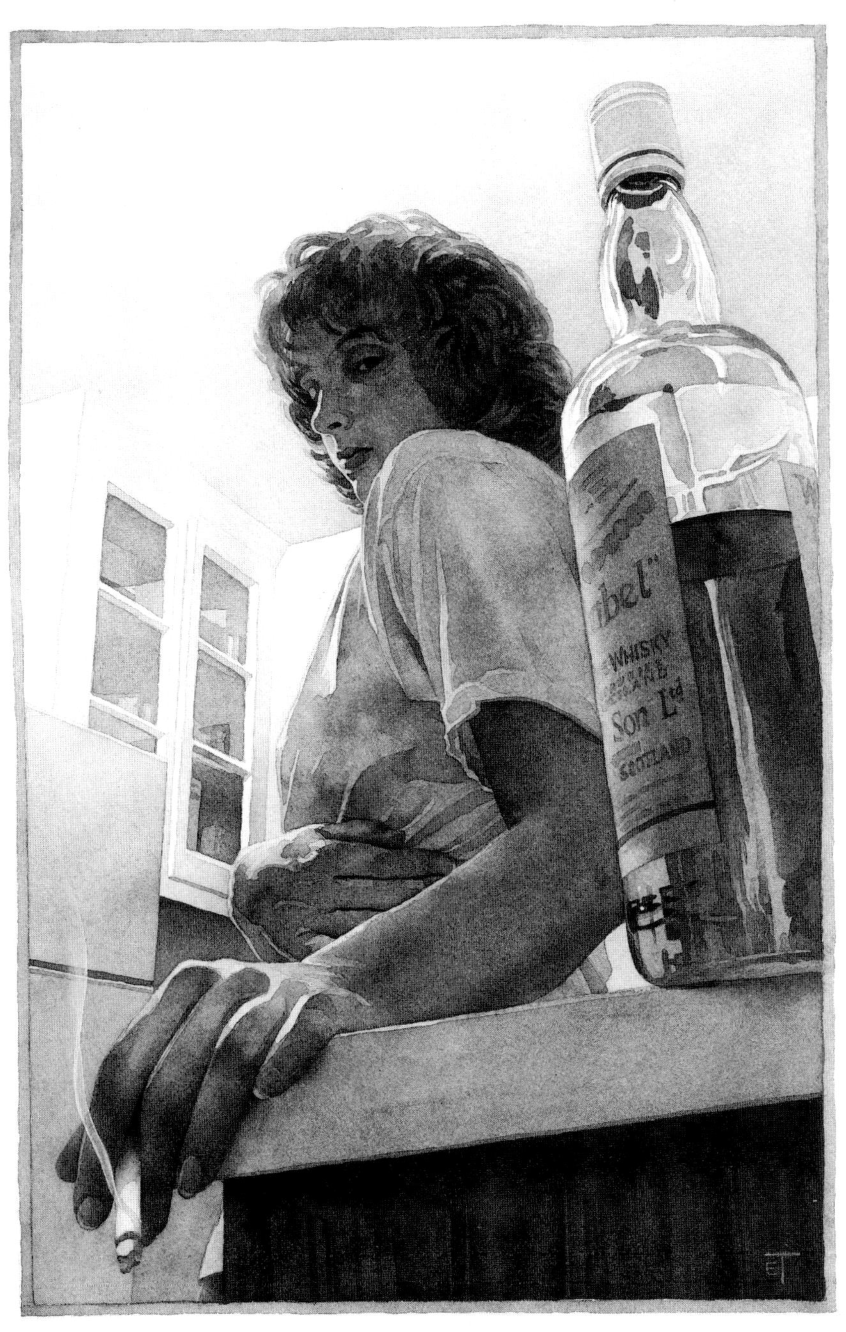

ELLEN THOMPSON
97 PINE GROVE AVE., SOMERSET, N.J. 08873
(908) 249-8640

NY Daily News

DANIEL ABRAHAM

718 •499 •4006
BOX 2528 • ROCKEFELLER CENTER STATION • NEW YORK, NEW YORK 10185
FAX IN STUDIO

PETER H. GILMORE
P.O. BOX 499, RADIO CITY STATION, NEW YORK, NY 10101–0499
(212) 245–2329

REPRESENTED BY MENDOLA LTD.
GRAYBAR BLDG., 420 LEXINGTON AVE., PENTHOUSE, NEW YORK, NY 10170
TELEPHONE (212) 986–5680 FAX (212) 818–1246

ART GLAZER

ART GLAZER
2 JAMES ROAD, MT. KISCO, N.Y. 10549
(914) 666–4554

Tropicana
PURE PREMIUM
Florida Squeezed
Orange Juice
FREE
Old Spice
Phil
Franké
REPRESENTED BY MENDOLA LTD.
(212) 986-5680-(516) 661-5778
FAX

·T·R·A·N·S·F·O

1. THE ASSIGNMENT.

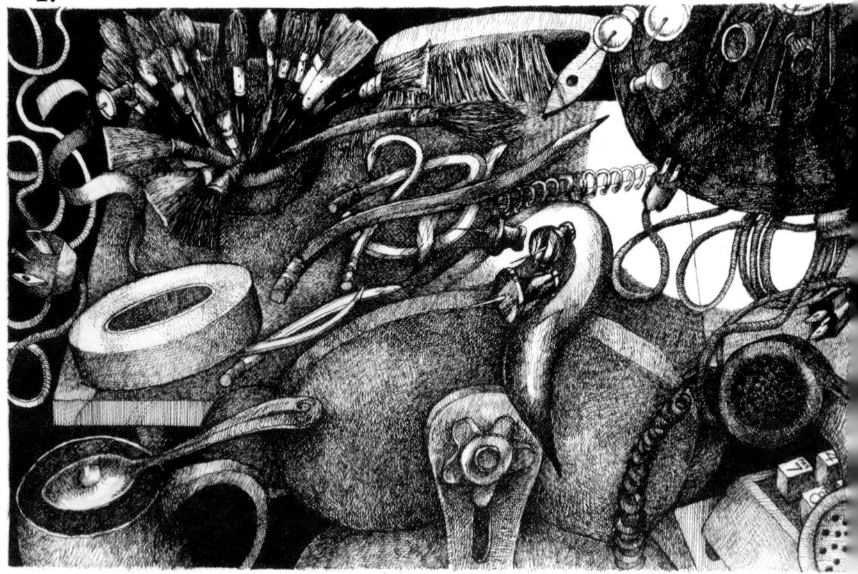

2. THE FIRST SKETCH.

R · M · A · T · I · O · N ·

THE DEADLINE APPROACHES.

THE REJECTION.

REPRESENTING

LORENZ · Schleh

VAN HOWELL (212) 621•9171 OR (516) 424•6499
CLIENTS: NY TIMES (ABOVE), NEWSDAY (TOP), DOW JONES, ESQUIRE, DOUBLEDAY
SEE ALSO RSVP 13–17, ILLUSTRATORS 26 & 32. COLOR OR B&W.

SERGE MICHAELS 11435 EMELITA ST. #1 NORTH HOLLYWOOD, CA 91601 818 / 753-1453

PETER WALLACE, 43 WACHUSETT ST., JAMAICA PLAIN, MA 02130 (617) 522-4917
CLIENTS INCLUDE: TV GUIDE, BOSTON HERALD, BOSTONIA MAGAZINE, D.C. HEATH, KING FEATURES, CAMPUS LIFE, KIDSPORTS.

BARBARA GRIFFEL

ILLUSTRATION; FASHION AND BEAUTY ILLUSTRATION
REALISTIC AND STYLIZED
(718) 631–1753

RANDALL RAYON

ILLUSTRATION

REPRESENTED BY CAROLYN BRINDLE, INC.
203 E. 89TH STREET, NEW YORK, NY 10128 • (212) 534-4177

REPRESENTED BY CAROLYN BRINDLE, INC.
203 E. 89TH STREET, NEW YORK, NY 10128 • (212) 534–4177

Reed Travel Group

Travel World

Della Femina McNamee Inc.

Nabisco Co.

American Express

CHRIS SPOLLEN "HIGH CONTRAS

Whittle Communications

Mother Jones Mag.

Womans Day Mag.

Money Saver

Nabisco Co

C.A. Design Group

CMP Pubs

Ogilvy & Mather Adv

ILLUSTRATION (718)·979-9695

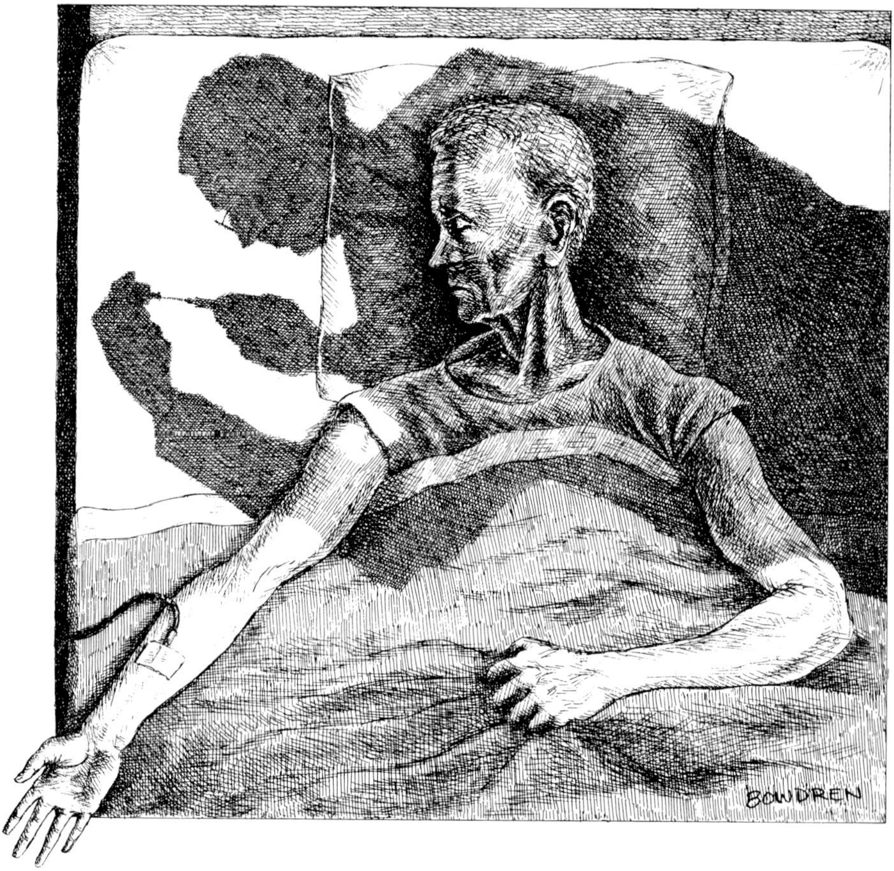

John Bowdren

FINISHED IDEAS IN BLACK AND WHITE OR COLOR
PORTFOLIO AND FAX AVAILABLE
RSVP CALLBACK ANSWERING SERVICE (718) 857-9267

(718) 788-1818

LINO CUTS • ENGRAVING • SCRATCHBOARD
CARBONE SMOLAN, FRANKLIN LIBRARY, NEW YORK TIMES
(718) 788–1818

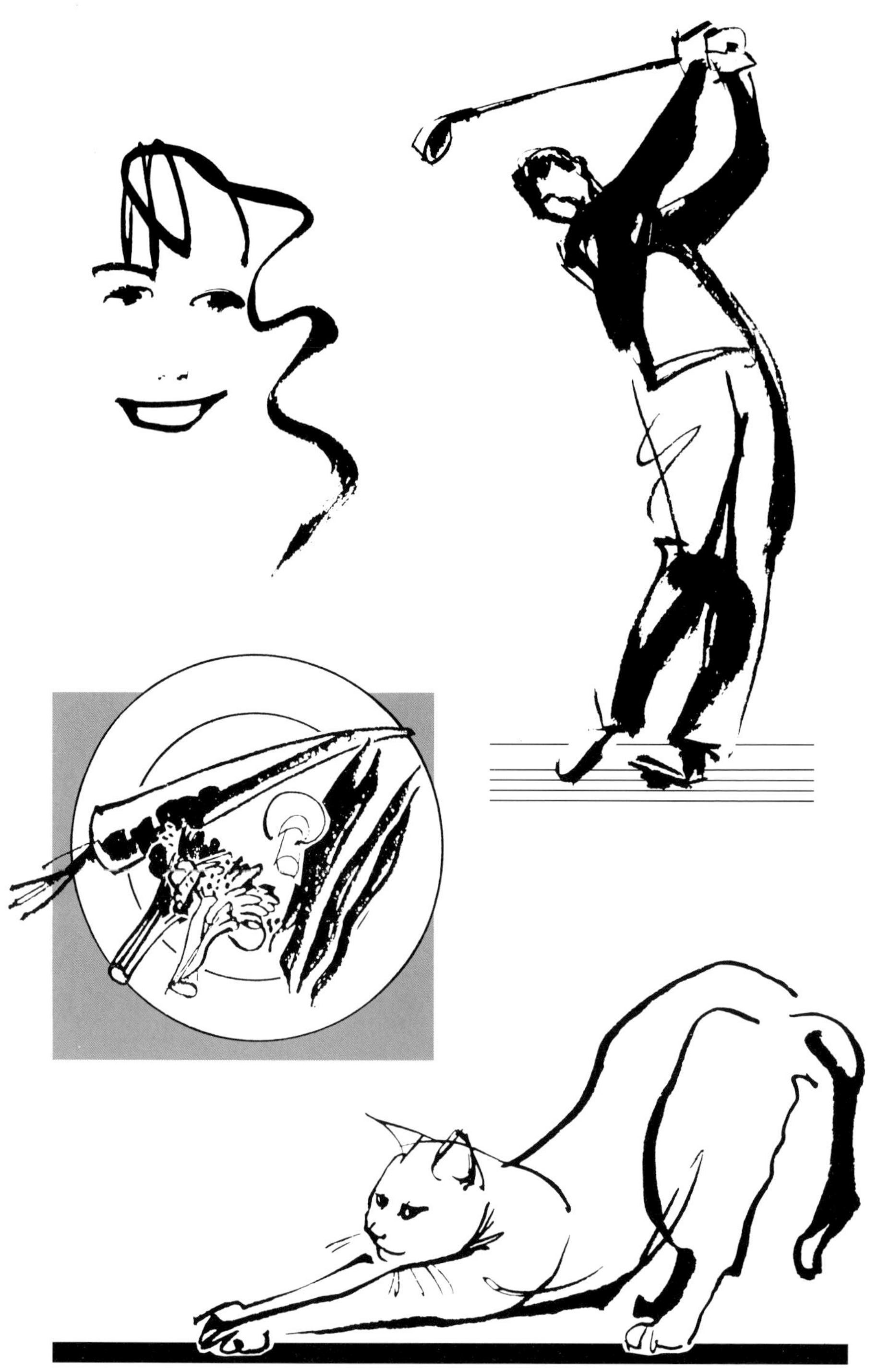

ROXANNE • PHONE 212-354-6641 • FAX 212-719-0377
CLIENTS INCLUDE LIZ CLAIBORNE, TIMES MIRROR CO., INSIDE SPORTS
ALSO SEE RSVP #15

Random House

The Calvert Group

DOROTHY LEECH • PHONE 212–354–6641 • FAX 212–719–0377

ALSO SEE RSVP #14 & 15, 1992 & 1993 CREATIVE ILLUSTRATION, AND DIRECTORY OF ILLUSTRATION #8

MARCY GOLD

35 FRIEDMAN RD., MONTICELLO, NY 12701
PHONE/FAX: (914) 794–0359

Katie Keller

KATIE KELLER ILLUSTRATION B&W/COLOR
33 SCHERMERHORN #3, BROOKLYN, NY 11201 TEL: (718) 522-2334

NEWYORKPOST
GODFATHER
RUBBED OUT
Slain outside midtown steak hou
NEWYORKP
NIGHTMAR
AT H
SH
HO

Mike Pearl crime reporter N.Y.

RICHARD TOMLINSON

(212) 685 0552 319 East 24th St., New York, N.Y. 10010

oo Centre St. NYC.

JILL RAPPAPORT OLIMB GRAFIX (619) 566-6247

WATERCOLOR • PENCIL • RAPIDOGRAPH • MIXED MEDIA
SPECIALIZING IN BOTANICALS AND ANIMALS
11454 ELBERT WAY • SAN DIEGO, CA 92126 • FAX (619) 566 • 3528

BIEGEL

BIEGEL

BIEGEL

BIEGEL

Laurie Harden

LAURIE HARDEN, 121 BANTA LANE, BOONTON, N.J. 07005 (201) 335-4578
CLIENTS: GROSSET & DUNLAP, AMERICAN LUNG ASSOC., ABC, CBS, NJ BELL N.Y. TIMES, LADIES HOME JOURNAL, SCHOLASTIC, RED BOOK, TIME INC.

SUSAN DETRICH · ILLUSTRATION

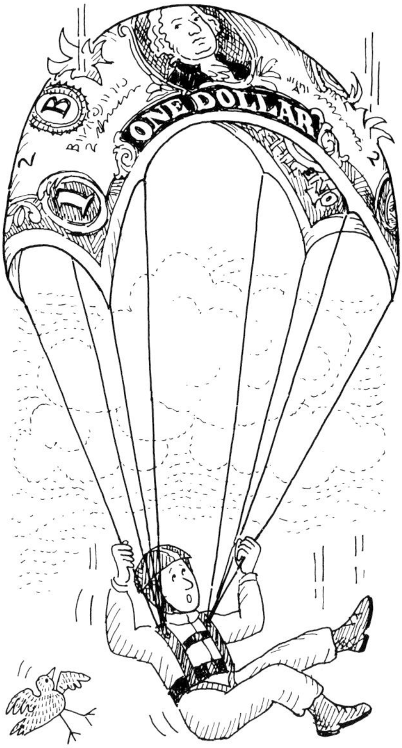

253 BALTIC STREET • BROOKLYN NEW YORK 11201 • 718–237–9174
FOR ADDITIONAL WORK SEE RSVP 16,17 • CREATIVE ILLUSTRATION BOOK 1991
& THE GRAPHIC ARTISTS GUILD'S DIRECTORY OF ILLUSTRATION 5•6•8•9

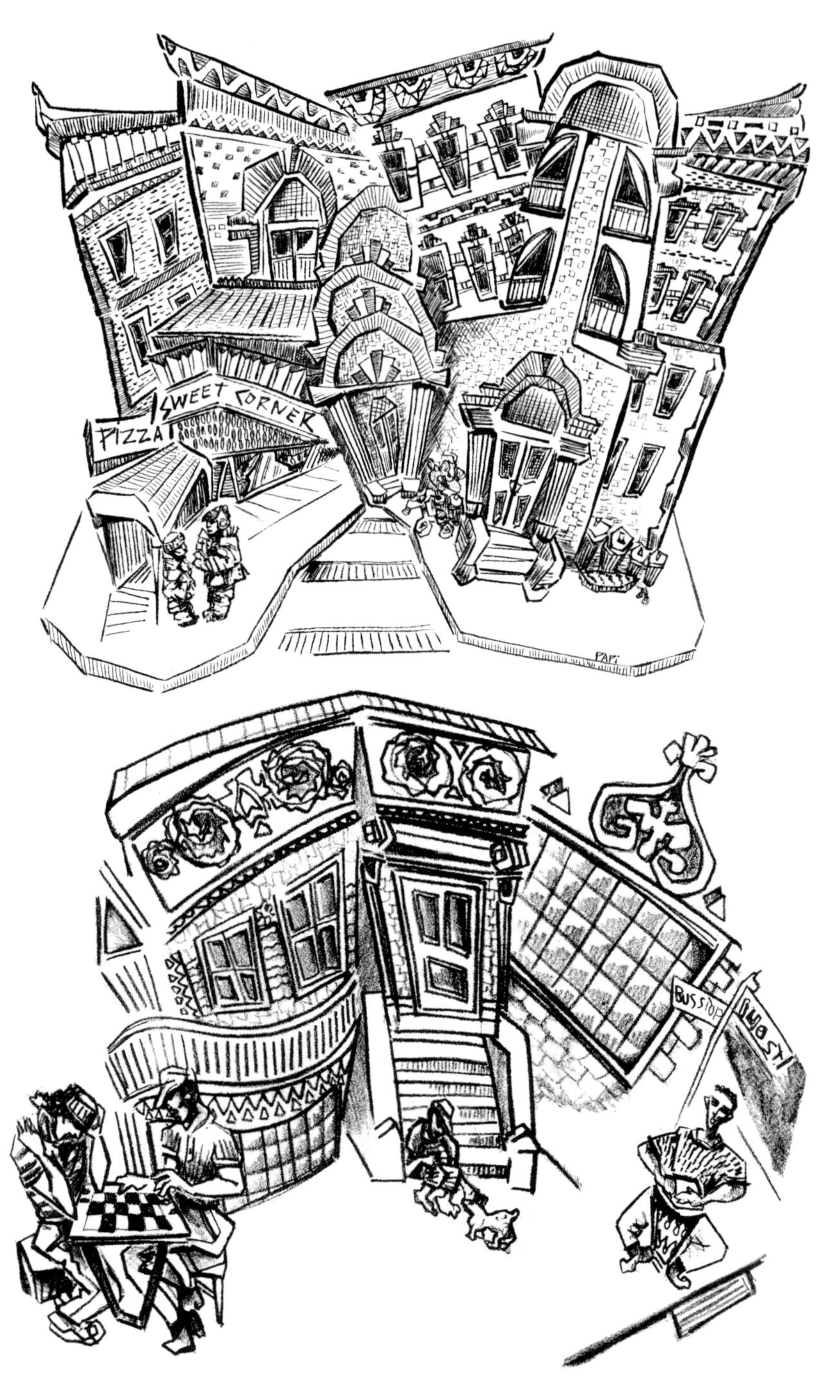

LIZA PAPI
LINE, WASH, WOODCUT, LITHO
231 W. 25TH ST., #3D, NEW YORK CITY 10001 212/627-7438

LORRAINE RABL

2 0 1 • 8 3 6 • 4 2 8 3

629 GLENWOOD AVENUE, TEANECK, NJ 07666

RSVP
THE DIRECTORY OF ILLUSTRATION AND DESIGN
18
MATTELSON

DESIGN

KEITH PIERRE LOGOS INC. (305) 726-0401
TYPOGRAPHIC SOLUTIONS FOR LOGOS, BOOK AND FILM TITLES
HEADLINES AND PACKAGING

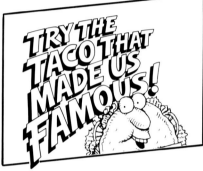

ISKRA JOHNSON

■ *Expressive Lettering & Typographic Design* ■

Hacienda

Auction of Northwest Wines

INTERNATIONAL THEATRE FESTIVAL OF CHICAGO

Fumé Blanc

Vin Rosé

THAILAND

(206) 323.8256 ■ FAX 323.6863

THAI AIRLINES, HELENE CURTIS, POLAROID, DOUBLEDAY, HARPER COLLINS, SIMON & SCHUSTER, PENGUIN USA, HYATT HOTELS, NINTENDO, AT&T, MCDONALD'S, ANHEUSER BUSCH, SONY MUSIC

Cheryl O. Adams

LETTERING ARTIST

High Quality

Fast Turnaround

CREATIVE

A·T·T·E·N·T·I·O·N T·O D·E·T·A·I·L

Flexible

DEPENDABLE

meets deadlines

• Reliable •

Enjoys Clients

CHERYL O. ADAMS
HAND LETTERING & DESIGN
TEL: (515) 223–7174 FAX: (515) 223–0654

Introducing the amazing new
Rave MoistureLock perms

NEWS 4 NEW YORK

Feeling
Pretty

PEOPLExpress

ABCDEFGHIJKLMNOPQRSTUVWXYZ

abcdefghijklmnopqrstuvwxyz

CRUZ & SLOWIK ASSOCIATES INC · 526 WEST 26 ST · NY NY 10001
Phone (212) 645-4600 · Fax (212) 645-4661 · Modem (212) 645-4702

We specialize in custom hand lettering, logotype designs, and creating beautiful typefaces. We're a fully equipped Macintosh computer design studio. Samples available upon request.

CARMINE VECCHIO • 212 683-2679 • 718 848-6176 • ANAGRAM DESIGN GROUP • NYC

IT'S AMAZING HOW SOME COMPUTER MANUFACTURERS INTERPRET USER FRIENDLY.

LOGOS, DESIGN & ILLUSTRATION • COMPUTER & COLOR AIRBRUSH

VISIONS

ANAGRAM DESIGN GROUP, NYC • LOGOS, DESIGN & UNUSUAL GRAPHICS • MACINTOSH OR MANUALLY CREATED

CARMINE VECCHIO • 212 683-2679 • 718 848-6176

LAURA KAY DESIGN

INTERNATIONAL AWARD–WINNING DESIGN
LOGOS • TRADEMARKS • CORPORATE IDENTITY PACKAGES
PHONE (800) 497–1752 • RSVP CALLBACK (718) 857–9267

PATRICK TOMASULO
76 HOWARD ST., DUMONT, NJ 07628 (201) 385•4350
GRAPHIC DESIGN • HANDLETTERING • AIRBRUSH

SINBAD
THE
VOYAGER

ANNE V. MACKECHNIE
HAND LETTERING & DESIGN FOR LOGOS • HEADLINES • ADVERTISING
PHONE & FAX 606/885-7883

MANAGEMENT
babywear
Summer Blonde
focus
Christina Estler
New Neutrals
THE TRUMPET CLUB
ORIGINAL·BOOK
Style
VERDIGRIS
Design
fashion
TIME WARNER
Studio·B
Soft Sculptures
Lipsticks
STILLWATER ASSOCIATES
PICK·OF·THE·HUNT
By Hand
LETTERING, LOGO AND SYMBOL DESIGN
A & S PLAZA • ARISTA RECORDS • ATLANTIC RECORDS • AVON • BANTAM • BLOOMINGDALE'S • BURSON MARSTELLAR
AIROL • CONRAN'S HABITAT • DELL BOOKS • DOUBLEDAY BOOKS • ESTEE LAUDER • FORTUNOFF • GITANO • GREY DIRECT
NDOR ASSOCIATES • LINTAS WORLDWIDE • LOWE MARSCHALK • MACY'S • MANHATTAN CABLE TV • MARK CROSS LEATHER
E COMMUNICATIONS • MCCANN-ERICKSON • MIDDLEBERG & ASSOCIATES • NATIONAL LAMPOON • NY PORT AUTHORITY
OPLE • PLAYBOY • RANDOM HOUSE • ROBERT LEE MORRIS • SAATCHI & SAATCHI • SCIENCE TIMES • TIME-WARNER
(212) 595-7737 FAX 874-6284

BUTLER DESIGNER SIGN COMPANY
4669 E. 900 N., SYRACUSE, IN 46567
(219) 457–2821 FAX (219) 457–2821 ATT: D. BUTLER

black white AND read
Inheret the Wind
Auntie Mame
CAUTION: EXPOSURE TO THE ELEMENTS WILL CAUSE
deterioration
SIX
EAST MAIN
AN OCCASION FOR BALLOONS
...BUT IS IT art ??
BEST Jewelry
MADE IN
USA
Quiver
ALLELUIA
LEWIS GINTER
BOTANICAL GARDEN
at Bloemendaal
SPECIAL
EFFEX

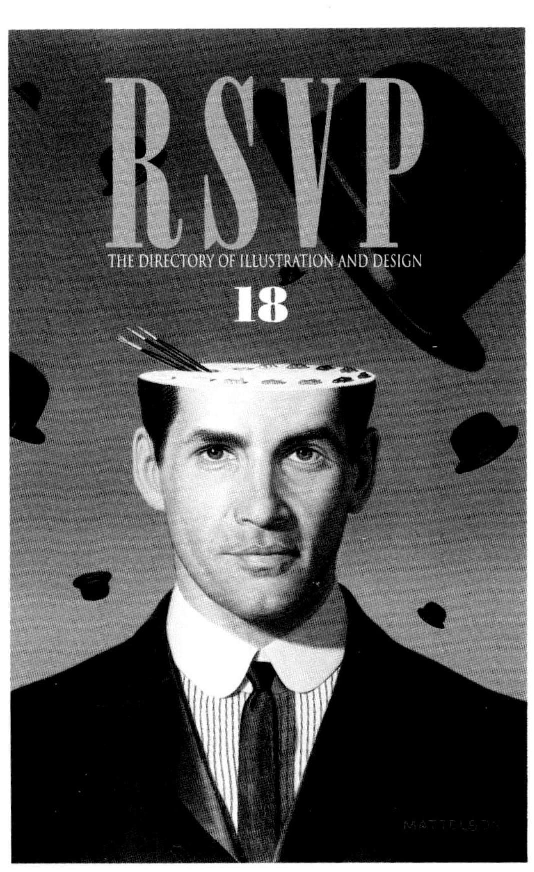

INDEX

ILLUSTRATION

ABRAHAM, Daniel E. (718) 499-4006 ... 242
ABRAMS, Edward (619) 544-9571, FAX (619) 544-0743 ... 59
AKGULIAN, Nishan (718) 565-6936 ... 132
ALLAN, Chris (718) 601-3743 * ... 192
AMICOSANTE, Vincent (408) 479-4803 * ... 85
ARCHAMBAULT, Matthew (516) 277-4722 ... 15
BAKER, Joe (212) 925-6555 ... 108,109
BARRETT, Ron (212) 874-1370 ... 44
BAUMAN, Jill (718) 886-5616 ... 18
BERG, Jeanne (516) 669-2366 ... 117
BERLIN, Rose Mary (914) 962-0526, FAX (914) 962-2266 ... 158
BERNARDIN, James (206) 771-1348 ... 35
BIEGEL, Michael David (201) 825-0084 ... 267
BJORKMAN, Steve (212) 490-2450, FAX (212) 697-6828 ... 31
BOWDREN, John * ... 258
BOZZINI, James (212) 490-2450, FAX (212) 697-6828 ... 30
BRACKEN, Carolyn (212) 254-4996, FAX (212) 995-0911 * ... 103
BRION, David (718) 858-0362, FAX (718) 596-4408 ... 49
BRUNKUS, Denise (908) 735-2671 ... 54
BUCALO, Ron (914) 332-0174 ... 116
BUCHART, Greta (203) 438-8386 ... 208
BUNNELL, Deb (215) 356-0362, FAX (215) 353-7531 ... 203
BUTLER DESIGNER SIGN CO. (219) 457-2821, FAX 457-2821 ... 286
CHAMBLESS WRIGHT, Jane (914) 368-8606 ... 189
CHUNG, Chi (203) 438-8386 ... 217
CLEMENT, Cameron (918) 621-5261 ... 46
COHEN, M.E. (212) 627-8033 ... 38
CONGE, Bob (716) 473-0291 ... 55
COOLEY, Rick (215) 356-0362, FAX (215) 353-7531 ... 205
COREY, Lee (617) 437-9459, FAX 437-6494, (401) 737-8591 ... 174
CORVI, Donna (212) 628-3102 ... 167
CRAWFORD, Emma (212) 420-1222, FAX (212) 673-5236 ... 184,185
CREIGHTON, Kathleen (718) 636-1111 * ... 87,88,89
CRUZ, Ray (914) 368-8696, (212) 475-0440 ... 188
CUDDY, Kevin (203) 325-9997, FAX (203) 359-6973 ... 168,169
CUDDY, Robbin (212) 254-4996, FAX (212) 995-0911 * ... 105
CUMMINGS, Terrance (212) 586-4193 ... 152,153
DEAL, Jim (212) 254-4996, FAX (212) 995-0911 * ... 94
DELAPINE, Jim (516) 225-1247 ... 27
DENHAM, Karl (201) 792-6422, FAX (201) 792-0658 ... 148
DETRICH, Susan (718) 237-9174 ... 269
DIDION, Nancy (617) 784-1389, FAX (617) 784-1391 ... 144
DOLOBOWSKY, Mena (800) 472-2047, (203) 222-1608 ... 80
DUGAN, Brian (908) 396-1231 ... 221
DUPONT, Lane (203) 222-1562 ... 50
DUTKO, Deborah (203) 925-0878 ... 143
DYEN, Don (215) 356-0362, FAX (215) 353-7531 ... 201
EBEL, Alex (914) 961-4058 ... 39
EBERT, Len (215) 356-0362, FAX (215) 353-7531 ... 200
EDWARDS, James (617) 437-9459, FAX 437-6494, (401) 737-8591 ... 172
EMBER, Kathy (212) 675-5719, FAX (212) 675-6341 ... 125
ENIK, Ted (212) 254-4996, FAX (212) 995-0911 * ... 102
ENRIC (212) 254-4996, FAX (212) 995-0911 * ... 93
ERICKSON, Richard (212) 675-5719, FAX (212) 675-6341 ... 129
ETTLINGER, Doris (908) 537-6322, FAX (908) 537-7966 ... 240
FAUST, Cliff (212) 581-9461 * ... 47

RSVP CallBack answering service (718) 857-9267

FISCHER, Karl (914) 737-5690 196
FLEETWOOD FINE ARTS/T. Giannotta (212) 924-4422 150,151
FLOCK ILLUSTRATION (708) 447-4454, FAX 447-0301 43
FRANK, Robert (914) 368-8606 190
FRANKE, Phil (212) 986-5680, (516) 661-5778 247
FREDRICKSON, Mark (602) 722-5777 24,25
FUJISAKI, Tuko (619) 494-5544 115
GALEY, Chuck (601) 373-6426, (214) 369-6990 68
GAMBLE, Kent ((212) 582-0023 145
GARDNER, Mike (617) 437-9459, FAX 437-6494, (401) 737-8591 173
GARRISON, Barbara (212) 348-6382 * 142
GARROW, Dan (212) 490-2450, FAX (212) 697-6828 28
GEARY, Rick (619) 544-9571, FAX (619) 544-0743 60
GHERARDI, Bob (609) 936-9138 166
GILMORE, Peter H. (212) 245-2329 244
GLAZER, Art (914) 666-4554 246
GOFFE, Toni (203) 438-8386 214
GOLD, Marcy (914) 794-0359 262
GOMEZ, Loretta (201) 656-5329, FAX (201) 656-5329 * 119
GRANT, Mel (212) 254-4996, FAX (212) 995-0911 * 95
GRAVES, Linda (203) 438-8386 215
GREENE, Jeffrey (203) 438-8386 210
GREGER, C. Shana (203) 438-8386 216
GREGORY, Lane (617) 235-8658 176
GRIFFEL, Barbara (718) 631-1753 253
GROSSMAN, Myron (212) 874-7074,(203) 222-1608,(818) 795-6992 83
GROTE, Rich (609) 586-5896 17
GURNEY, John Steven (718) 462-5073 * 16
GYURCSAK, Joe (609) 586-7007 162
HAEFELE, Steve (212) 254-4996, FAX (212) 995-0911 * 96
HANNON, Holly (212) 254-4996, FAX (212) 995-0911 * 100
HARDEN, Laurie (201) 335-4578 268
HARRINGTON, Stephen (203) 226-4724, FAX 454-9904 236,237
HARTER, Jim * 63
HENRY, Steve (212) 532-2487 77
HERGERT, Greg * 66
HOBBS, Bill (919) 282-2377 106
HOEFFNER, Deb (201) 838-5490 139
HOLDER, John (215) 356-0362, FAX (215) 353-7531 204
HOWELL, Van (212) 621-9171, (516) 424-6499 250
HUFFMAN, Tom (212) 819-0211 149
IOSA, Ann W. (203) 438-8386 212
ISKOWITZ, Joel (203) 438-8386 209
JOBE, Jody (212) 795-4941 * 197
JOHNSON, Joanne (516) 781-7593 238
JOHNSON, Larry (617) 235-8658 177
JUNG, Rodney (718) 544-4278, FAX (718) 544-3341 37
KASTNER, John (617) 437-9459, FAX 437-6494, (401) 737-8591 175
KEETER, Susan (212) 675-5719, FAX (212) 675-6341 130
KELLER, Katie (718) 522-2334 263
KENNEDY, Anne (212) 675-5719, FAX (212) 675-6341 126
KING, Manuel (617) 437-9459, FAX 437-6494, (401) 737-8591 170
KLEIN, David G. (718) 788-1818 259
KLEMENTZ-HARTE, Lauren (203) 235-6145 133
KOSTER, Aaron (908) 536-2815 193
KRIEGER, Salem (201) 963-3754, FAX (201) 963-3754 48
KROVATIN, Dan (617) 235-8658 178
KUCHARSKI, Michael (313) 283-4324 111

RSVP CallBack answering service (718) 857-9267

LAPADULA, Tom (212) 254-4996, FAX (212) 995-0911 * 98
LACKOW, Andy (201) 854-2770 33
LADEN, Nina (404) 371-0052, (800) 743-5196 160
LANG, Cecily (212) 580-3424 * 198
LEBENSON, Richard (718) 857-9267 234,235
LEECH, Dorothy (212) 354-6641, FAX (212) 840-9452 261
LEMANT, Albert (212) 675-5719, FAX (212) 675-6341 131
LESTER, Mike (706) 234-7733, FAX (706) 234-7594 40,41
LIGASAN, Darryl (212) 722-8926 * 65
LORENZ STUDIO, Albert (516) 354-5530 248,249
LOVELL, Rick (404) 8442-3943, FAX (404) 475-8321 14
LUSTIG, Loretta (718) 789-2496....................135
MACNEILL, Scott (609) 397-4631....................243
MANTHA, Nancy (203) 438-8386 211
MARTIN, Richard (516) 377-3844 26
MARTINEZ, Sergio (212) 254-4996, FAX (212) 995-0911 * 99
MARTINOT, Claude (212) 473-3137, 212) 645-0097 164
MARVIN, Fred (212) 254-4996, FAX (212) 995-0911 * 97
MARZIALI, Sandra (212) 874-7074, (203) 222-1608 81
MATTELSON, Marvin (212) 684-2974 21
MCCLURE, Tim (214) 905-9037, FAX (214) 905-9038....................52
MCMAHON, Peter (718) 625-1264 * 163
MEAD, Kimble (718) 768-3632 75
MEHALKO, Donna (212) 534-4177....................255
MEISEL, Paul (212) 675-5719, FAX (212) 675-6341....................124
MERRILEES, Rebecca A. (215) 356-0362, FAX (215) 353-7531....................202
MICHAELS, Serge (818) 753-1453 84,251
MILES, Chris (718) 499-1656 * 67
MILGRIM, David (212) 673-1432....................42
MINOR, Wendell (203) 868-9101, FAX (203) 868-9512 45
MOSCOWITZ, Stephen (617)437-9459,FAX 437-6494,(401)737-8591 171
MUELCHI, Jannine (619) 943-1196, FAX (619) 943-7412....................114
MYERS GRAPHICS, David (212) 989-5260....................220
MYERS, V. Gene (201) 429-8131 134
NAPOLI, Augie (718) 356-0513, (212) 337-6142 165
O'MALLEY, Kathleen (617) 235-8658....................179
O'MALLEY, Kevin (914) 368-8606....................191
OLIMB GRAFIX/Robin Olimb, J.Rappaport (619) 566-6247 78,266
PALMER, Jan (212) 675-5719, FAX (212) 675-6341 123
PAPI, Liza (212) 627-7438....................270
PARADA, Roberto (201) 998-0922 112
PARRY, Ivor (212) 779-1554, FAX (212) 447-7848 187
PEPPER, Bob (718) 875-3236....................23
PHILLIPS, Gary (617) 235-8658 181
POLENGHI, Evan (718) 499-3214, (212) 966-9897 154
PUNCHATZ, Don Ivan (817) 469-8151, (212) 989-7074 20
RABL, Lorraine (201) 836-4283....................271
RAPPAPORT, Jill/Olimb Grafix (619) 566-6247, FAX 566-3528 266
RAYON, Randall (212) 534-4177 254
REED, Chris (908) 548-3927, (908) 603-0842 107
REINGOLD, Alan (212) 697-6170 13
REINHARDT, Dorothy (415) 584-9369 * 64
RICCIO, Frank (212) 986-5680, FAX (212) 818-1246 245
ROBERTS, Scott (410) 366-0737 86
ROBERTS, Tom (201) 347-7743 32
ROBINSON, Anthony Valentino * 22
ROMAN, Barbara (212) 362-1374....................156
ROMER, Dan V. (718) 789-8442....................79

RSVP CallBack answering service (718) 857-9267

ROPER, Robert * 34
ROSALES, Melodye (212) 254-4996, FAX (212) 995-0911 * 101
ROUNDY, Laine (203) 426-9531, FAX (203) 270-7223 155
ROXANNE (212) 354-6641, FAX (212) 840-9452 260
SALEM, Kay (214) 905-9037, FAX (214) 905-9038 53
SANJULIAN (212) 254-4996, FAX (212) 995-0911 * 92
SANO, Kazuhiko (212) 490-2450, FAX (212) 697-6828 29
SCHEUER, Philip A. (212) 620-0728 74
SCHMIDT, George P. (718) 857-1837 157
SHIELDS, Sandy S. (203) 438-8386 207
SILVERS, Bill (216) 899-1906 * 118
SMITH, Mark T. (212) 673-8446 147
SOFO, Frank R. (516) 681-8745 * 90
SOILEAU, Hodges (203) 852-0751, FAX (203) 831-9155 36
SOLOMON, Debra (212) 924-7014, FAX (212) 924-3228 159
SOPER, Pat (617) 235-8658 180
SOURS, Michael (214) 905-9037, FAX (214) 905-9038 51
SPELLMAN, Susan (617) 235-8658 182
SPENGLER, Ken (212) 865-0692, (916) 441-1932 56,57
SPOLLEN, Chris (718) 979-9695 256,257
STATON, Maggie (203) 438-8386 213
STEWART, April Blair (800) 472-2047, (203) 222-1608 82
STROMOSKI, Rick (203) 668-8738, FAX (203) 668-8742 186
SWENY, Stephen (310) 823-0095 * 71
TAGEL, Peggy (212) 675-5719, FAX (212) 675-6341 128
TALARO, Lionel (619) 544-9571, FAX (619) 544-0743 61
TAYLOR, B.K. (313) 626-8698, (212) 243-1333 69
TEXEIRA, Mark (914) 337-2286 * 91
THOMPSON, Darren (317) 641-7046 239
THOMPSON, Ellen (908) 249-8640 241
THOMPSON, Emily (718) 937-2388 * 161
THOMPSON, George (718) 937-2388 * 141
THOMPSONS, The (212) 254-4996, FAX (212) 995-0911 * 104
TILLERY, Angelo (718) 617-2907 * 62,233
TOMLINSON, Richard (212) 685-0552 264,265
TORRES, Carlos (718) 768-3296 146
TORRISI, Gary (617) 235-8658 183
VAN MUNCHING, Paul * 120,121
VELASQUEZ, Eric (212) 316-3657 * 110
VELEZ, Walter (718) 886-5616 19
VELTFORT, Anna (212) 877-0430 140
VEROUGSTRAETE, Randy (212) 675-5719, FAX (212) 675-6341 127
WALDMAN, Bruce (718) 846-6411 * 138
WALDMAN, Bryna (212) 929-2951, (201) 568-4868 206
WALLACE, Peter B. (617) 522-4917 252
WATTS, Sharon (718) 398-0451 76
WENZEL, David (212) 675-5719, FAX (212) 675-6341 122
WHITEHEAD, S.B. (212) 686-5250, (718) 768-0803 70
WILLIAMS, Elizabeth (212) 945-6442 194,195
WOLEK, Guy (918) 451-2546 58
YALOWITZ, Paul * 113
YEE, Josie (212) 206-1260, FAX (212) 627-6674 136,137
YERKES, Lane (215) 356-0362, FAX (215) 353-7531 199
ZIMMERMAN, Robert (718) 237-0699 72,73

RSVP CallBack answering service (718) 857-9267

FASHION ILLUSTRATION/ACCESSORIES

CORVI, Donna (212) 628-3102 167
GRIFFEL, Barbara (718) 631-1753 253
MEHALKO, Donna (212) 534-4177 255
RAYON, Randall (212) 534-4177 254
WILLIAMS, Elizabeth (212) 945-6442 194,195

3D ILLUSTRATION

OLIMB GRAFIX/Robin Olimb (619) 566-6247, FAX 566-3528 78

COLLAGE

FAUST, Cliff (212) 581-9461 * 47
HARTER, Jim * 63
MARTINOT, Claude (212) 473-3137, (212) 645-0097 164
OLIMB GRAFIX/Robin Olimb (619) 566-6247, FAX 566-3528 78
ROMER, Dan V. (718) 789-8442 79
TAGEL, Peggy (212) 675-5719, FAX (212) 675-6341 128
WATTS, Sharon (718) 398-0451 76

SILHOUETTES & CUT-OUTS

CRAWFORD, Emma (212) 420-1222, FAX (212) 673-5236 184,185
FAUST, Cliff (212) 581-9461 * 47
GOLD, Marcy (914) 794-0359 262
LANG, Cecily (212) 580-3424 * 198
MARTINOT, Claude (212) 473-3137, (212) 645-0097 164
SPOLLEN, Chris (718) 979-9695 256,257
TAGEL, Peggy (212) 675-5719, FAX (212) 675-6341 128

WOOD-CUTS/SCRATCHBOARD

CLEMENT, Cameron (918) 621-5261 46
FLOCK ILLUSTRATION (708) 447-4454, FAX (708) 447-0301 43
KELLER, Katie ((718) 522-2334 263
KLEIN, David G. (718) 788-1818 259
KROVATIN, Dan (617) 235-8658 178
LEECH, Dorothy (212) 354-6641, FAX (212) 840-9452 261
MUELCHI, Jannine (619) 943-1196, FAX (619) 943-7412 114
PAPI, Liza (212) 627-7438 270
REINHARDT, Dorothy (415) 584-9369 * 64
RICCIO, Frank (212) 986-5680, FAX (212) 818-1246 245
ZIMMERMAN, Robert (718) 237-0699 72,73

CARTOONING/HUMOROUS

ABRAHAM, Daniel E. (718) 499-4006 242
AKGULIAN, Nishan (718) 565-6936 132
ALLAN, Chris (718) 601-3743 * 192
BARRETT, Ron (212) 874-1370 44
BJORKMAN, Steve (212) 490-2450, FAX (212) 697-6828 31

BRION, David (718) 858-0362, FAX (718) 596-4408 49
BRUNKUS, Denise (908) 735-2671 54
BUCALO, Ron (914) 332-0174 116
BUCHART, Greta (203) 438-8386 208
COHEN, M.E. (212) 627-8033 38
CONGE, Bob (716) 473-0291 55
CORY, Lee (617) 437-9459, FAX 437-6494, (401) 737-8591 174
CUDDY, Robbin (212) 254-4996, FAX (212) 995-0911 * 105
DENHAM, Karl (201) 792-6422, FAX (201) 792-0658 148
DETRICH, Susan (718) 237-9174 269
DOLOBOWSKY, Mena (800) 472-2047, (203) 222-1608 80
FISCHER, Karl (914) 737-5690 196
FREDRICKSON, Mark (602) 722-5777 24,25
FUJISAKI, Tuko (619) 494-5544 115
GALEY, Chuck (601) 373-6426, (214) 369-6990 68
GAMBLE, Kent (212) 582-0023 145
GARROW, Dan (212) 490-2450, FAX (212) 697-6828 28
GEARY, Rick (619) 544-9571, FAX (619) 544-0743 60
GLAZER, Art (914) 666-4554 246
GOMEZ, Loretta (201) 656-5329, FAX (201) 656-5329 * 119
GROSSMAN, Myron (212) 874-7074, (203) 222-1608, (818) 795-6992 83
GURNEY, John Steven (718) 462-5073 * 16
HENRY, Steve (212) 532-2487 77
HOBBS, Bill (919) 282-2377 106
HOWELL, Van (212) 621-9171, (516) 424-6499 250
HUFFMAN, Tom (212) 819-0211 149
JOBE, Jody (212) 795-4941 * 197
JOHNSON Joanne C. (516) 781-7593 238
KASTNER, John (617) 437-9459, FAX 437-6494, (401) 737-8591 175
KENNEDY, Anne (212) 675-5719, FAX (212) 675-6341 126
KING, Manuel (617) 437-9459, FAX 437-6494, (401) 737-8591 170
KOSTER, Aaron (908) 536-2815 193
LACKOW, Andy (201) 854-2770 33
LADEN, Nina (404) 371-0052, (800) 743-5196 160
LESTER, Mike (706) 234-7733, FAX (706) 234-7594 40,41
LORENZ STUDIO, Albert (516) 354-5530 248,249
LUSTIG, Loretta (718) 789-2496 135
MARVIN, Fred (212) 254-4996, FAX (212) 995-0911 * 97
MCMAHON, Peter (718) 625-1264 * 163
MEAD, Kimble Pendleton (718) 768-3632 75
MEISEL, Paul (212) 675-5719, FAX (212) 675-6341 124
MILGRIM, David (212) 673-1432 42
MUELCHI, Jannine (619) 943-1196, FAX (619) 943-7412 114
MYERS, V. Gene (201) 429-8131 134
NAPOLI, Augie (718) 356-0513, (212) 337-6142 165
OLIMB GRAFIX/Robin Olimb (619) 566-6247, FAX 566-3528 78
PARRY, Ivor (212) 779-1554, FAX (212) 447-7848 187
REED, Chris (908) 548-3927, FAX (908) 603-0842 * 107
SCHEUER, Philip A. (212) 620-0728 74
SOLOMON, Debra (212) 924-7014, FAX (212) 924-3228 159
SOURS, Michael (214) 905-9037, FAX (214) 905-9038 51
STROMOSKI, Rick (203) 668-8738, FAX (203) 668-8742 186
SWENY, Stephen (310) 823-0095 * 71
TAYLOR, B.K. (313) 626-8698, (212) 243-1333 69
THOMPSON, Emily (718) 937-2388 * 161
THOMPSON, George (718) 937-2388 * 141
THOMPSONS, The (212) 254-4996, FAX 212) 995-0911 * 104
VELTFORT, Anna (212) 877-0430 140

RSVP CallBack answering service (718) 857-9267

VEROUGSTRAETE, Randy (212) 675-5719, FAX (212) 675-6341 127
WALLACE, Peter B. (617) 522-4917 252
YALOWITZ, Paul * 113
YEE, Josie (212) 206-1260, FAX (212) 627-6674 136,137
YERKES, Lane (215) 356-0362, FAX (215) 353-7531 199
ZIMMERMAN, Robert (718) 237-0699 72,73

CARICATURES

BUCALO, Ron (914) 332-0174 116
FREDRICKSON, Mark (602) 722-5777 24,25
GAMBLE, Kent (212) 582-0023 145
HAEFELE, Steve (212) 254-4996, FAX (212) 995-0911 * 96
HOWELL, Van (212) 621-9171, (516) 424-6499 250
NAPOLI, Augie (718) 356-0513, (212) 337-6142 165
PARADA, Roberto (201) 998-0922 112
PEPPER, Bob (718) 875-3236 23
ROBINSON, Anthony Valentino * 22
SWENY, Stephen (310) 823-0095 * 71
TORRES, Carlos (718) 768-3296 146
THOMPSON, Darren (317) 641-7046 239
WHITEHEAD, S.B. (212) 686-5250, (718) 768-0803 70

COMIC ART

WALLACE, Peter B. (617) 522-4917 252

COURTROOM ART

TOMLINSON, Richard (212) 685-0552 264,265
WILLIAMS, Elizabeth (212) 945-6442 194,195

COMPS & STORYBOARDS

FRANKE, Phil (212) 986-5680, (516) 661-5778 247

ANIMATION

BJORKMAN, Steve (212) 490-2450, FAX (212) 697-6828 31
FISCHER, Karl (914) 737-5690 196
SOLOMON, Debra (212) 924-7014, FAX (212) 924-3228 159

ARCHITECTURAL RENDERING & ILLUSTRATION

BIEGEL, Michael David (201) 825-0084 267
LORENZ STUDIO, Albert (516) 354-5530 248,249

TECHNICAL RENDERING & PRODUCT ILLUSTRATION

ANAGRAM DESIGN (718) 848-6176, (212) 683-2679 225,280,281

RSVP CallBack answering service (718) 857-9267

CORVI, Donna (212) 628-3102 167
FRANKE, Phil (212) 986-5680, (516) 661-5778....................247
GOLD, Marcy (914) 794-0359 262
GROTE, Rich (609) 586-5896 17
HARRINGTON, Stephen (203) 226-4724, FAX 454-9904....................236,237
KRIEGER, Salem (201) 963-3754, FAX (201) 963-3754 48
MARTINOT, Claude (212) 473-3137, (212) 645-0097 164
MATTELSON, Marvin (212) 684-2974....................21
MOSCOWITZ, Stephen (617)437-9459,FAX437-6494,(401)737-8591 171
PUNCHATZ, Don Ivan (817) 469-8151, (212) 989-7074 20
ROMAN, Barbara (212) 362-1374....................156
ROPER, Robert * 34
TOMLINSON, Richard (212) 685-0552 264,265
TORRISI, Gary (617) 235-8658....................183

SCIENTIFIC ILLUSTRATION

MERRILEES, Rebecca A. (215) 356-0362, FAX (215) 353-7531....................202
RAPPAPORT, Jill/Olimb Grafix (619) 566-6247, FAX 566-3528 266
TORRISI, Gary (617) 235-8658....................183

CHARTS & MAPS

GRAPHIC CHARTS & MAP CO. (212) 463-0190 228,229

COMPUTER ART

ANAGRAM DESIGN (718) 848-6176, (212) 683-2679 225,280,281
BODKIN DESIGN GROUP (203) 221-0404, FAX (203) 221-1181....................226
BY HAND DESIGN (212) 595-7737, FAX 874-6284....................285
CRUZ & SLOWIK ASSOC. INC. (212) 645-4600, FAX 645-4661 279
GRAPHIC CHART & MAP CO. (212) 463-0190 228,229
GROSSMAN, Myron (212) 874-7074, (203) 222-1608, (818) 795-6992 83
MACNEILL, Scott (609) 397-4631....................243

ARTISTS REPRESENTATIVES

AMERICAN ARTISTS (212) 682-2462, (212) 582-0023.................... 145
BAHM, Bob (216) 398-1338....................20
BAHM, Darwin (212) 989-7074....................20
BANCROFT & FRIENDS, Carol (203) 438-8386 207-217
BAUMAN, Jill (718) 886-5616....................18,19
BERANBAUM, Sheryl (617) 437-9459, (401) 737-8591 170-175
BREWSTER CREATIVE SERVICES, John (203) 226-4724....................236,237
BRINDLE, Carolyn (212) 534-4177 254,255
CONLON, Jean (212) 966-9897....................154
FISHBACK, Lee (212) 929-2951, (201) 568-4868 206
GOLDSTEIN, Gwen Walters (617) 235-8658 176-183
GRIEN, Anita (212) 697-6170....................13
GYURCSAK, Lisa (609) 586-7007....................162
HK PORTFOLIO/Harriet Kasak (212) 675-5719, FAX 675-6341 122-131
IVY LEAGUE OF ARTISTS/Ivy Mindlin (212) 243-1333....................69
KELLY NEAIL ASSOCIATES (212) 865-0692, (916) 441-1932 56,57
MATTELSON, Judy (212) 684-2974....................21

RSVP CallBack answering service (718) 857-9267

MCCANN CO., The (214) 871-0353 145
MENDOLA LTD. (212) 986-5680 245,247
MORGAN ASSOCIATES, Vicki (212) 475-0440 188
RENARD REPRESENTS, (212) 490-2450, FAX (212) 697-6828....28-31
REPERTOIRE/Andrea Lynch (214) 369-6990 68
ROMAN ASSOCIATES, Helen (800) 472-2047, (203) 222-1608 80-83
S.I.INTERNATIONAL/Herb Spiers (212)254-4996,FAX995-0911 92-105
SANDS, Trudy (214) 905-9037, FAX (214) 905-9038 51-53
SCROGGY, David (619) 544-9571, FAX (619) 544-0743 59-61
TURK, Melissa (Artist Network) (914) 368-8606 188-191
VELORIC, Philip (215) 356-0362, FAX 353-7531 199-205

GRAPHIC DESIGN

ADAMS, Cheryl O. (515) 223-7174, FAX (515) 223-0654 278
ANAGRAM DESIGN GROUP (718) 848-6176,(212) 683-2679 225,280,28
BAUMAN, Jill (718) 886-5616....18
BLEIWEISS DESIGN, Richard (516) 679-9391 227
BODKIN DESIGN GROUP (203) 221-0404, FAX (203) 221-1181....226
BUTLER DESIGNER SIGN CO. (219) 457-2821, FAX 457-2821 286
BY HAND DESIGN (212) 595-7737, FAX 874-6284....285
CLARK, Michael * 287
CRAWFORD, Emma (212) 420-1222, FAX (212) 673-5236 184,185
CREIGHTON, Kathleen (718) 636-1111 * 87,88,89
CRUZ & SLOWIK ASSOC. INC. (212) 645-4600, FAX 645-4661 279
FLEETWOOD DESIGN/T. Giannotta (212) 924-4422 224
GIANNOTTA, Tommaso (212) 924-4422....224
KAY DESIGN, Laura (800) 497-1752 * 282
MACKECHNIE, Anne V. (606) 885-7883....284
MYERS GRAPHICS, David (212) 989-5260 220
NIKOSEY, Tom (818) 704-9993, FAX (818) 704-9995....222,223
PARRY, Ivor (212) 779-1554, FAX (212) 447-7848....187
REED, Chris (908) 548-3927, FAX (908) 603-0842....107
THE WRITE DIRECTION (706) 546-5058 * 276
TOMASULO, Patrick (201) 385-4350 283

LETTERING, LOGOS & CALLIGRAPHY

ADAMS, Cheryl O. (515) 223-7174, FAX (515) 223-0654 278
ANAGRAM DESIGN GROUP (718) 848-6176,(212) 683-2679....225,280,281
BODKIN DESIGN GROUP (203) 221-0404, FAX (203) 221-1181....226
BUTLER DESIGNER SIGN CO. (219) 457-2821, FAX 457-2821 286
BY HAND DESIGN (212) 595-7737, FAX 874-6284....285
CLARK, Michael * 287
CRUZ & SLOWIK ASSOC. INC. (212) 645-4600, FAX 645-4661 279
DUGAN DESIGN, Brian (908) 396-1231 221
FLEETWOOD DESIGN/T.Giannotta (212) 924-4422 224
JOHNSON, Iskra (206) 323-8256, FAX 323-6863 277
KAY DESIGN, Laura (800) 497-1752 * 282
MACKECHNIE, Anne V. (606) 885-7883....284
MYERS GRAPHICS, David (212) 989-5260 220
NIKOSEY, Tom (818) 704-9993, FAX (818) 704-9995....222,223
PIERRE, Keith (305) 726-0401....275
THE WRITE DIRECTION (706) 546-5058 * 276
TOMASULO, Patrick (201) 385-4350 283
VECCHIO, Carmine (718) 848-6176,(212) 683-2679 225,280,281

RSVP CallBack answering service (718) 857-9267

ART DIRECTION

ANAGRAM DESIGN GROUP (718) 848-6176,(212) 683-2679.....225,280,281
BLEIWEISS DESIGN, Richard (516) 679-9391 227
BODKIN DESIGN GROUP (203) 221-0404, FAX (203) 221-1181.....226
BY HAND DESIGN (212) 595-7737, FAX 874-6284.....285
MACKECHNIE, Anne V. (606) 885-7883.....284

PACKAGE DESIGN

ANAGRAM DESIGN GROUP (718) 786-2020,(212) 683-2679.....225,280,281
BLEIWEISS DESIGN, Richard (516) 679-9391 227
BODKIN DESIGN GROUP (203) 221-0404, FAX (203) 221-1181.....226
ROMAN, Barbara (212) 362-1374 156

HAND-PAINTED PHOTOGRAPHY

BAKER, Joe (212) 925-6555 108,109
CREIGHTON, Kathleen (718) 636-1111 * 87,88,89

GEOGRAPHIC BREAKDOWN

NEW ENGLAND (CT ME MA NH RI VT)

BANCROFT, Carol (Rep), Ridgefield, CT 207-217
BERANBAUM, Sheryl (Rep), Warwick, RI 170-175
BODKIN DESIGN GROUP (Des), Westport, CT 226
BOWDREN, John (Illus), Freeport, ME 258
BREWSTER, John (Rep), Westport, CT....236,237
CUDDY, Kevin (Illus), Stamford, CT 168-169
DIDION, Nancy (Illus), Sharon, MA....144
DUPONT, Lane (Illus), Westport, CT 50
DUTKO, Deborah (Illus), Huntington, CT 143
GOLDSTEIN, Gwen Walters (Rep), Wellesley, MA....176-183
HARRINGTON, Stephen (Illus), Norwalk, CT....236,237
IOSA, Ann (Illus), Southbury, CT 212
KLEMENTZ-HARTE, Lauren (Illus), Meriden, CT 133
MEISEL, Paul (Illus), Brookfield, CT 124
MERRILEES, Rebecca (Illus), Northfield, VT 202
MINOR, Wendell (Illus), Washington, CT....45
RICCIO, Frank (Illus), West Redding, CT....245
ROMAN, Helen (Rep), Weston, CT....80-83
ROUNDY, Laine (Illus), Sandy Hook, CT 155
SHIELDS, Sandy S. (Illus), Bristol, RI....207
SOILEAU, Hodges (Illus), Norwalk, CT 36
STROMOSKI, Rick (Illus), Suffield, CT 186
TORRISI, Gary (Illus), Methuen, MA 183
WALLACE, Peter B. (Illus), Jamaica Plains, MA 252
WENZEL, David (Illus), Durham, CT 122

MIDDLE ATLANTIC (DE DC MD NY & NJ [exclusive of GreaterMetro. Area] PA WV)

BERLIN, Rose Mary (Illus), Yorktown Heights, NY 158
BRUNKUS, Denise (Illus), Pittstown, NJ 54
BUCHART, Greta (Illus), Willow Grove, PA 208
CONGE, Bob (Illus), Rochester, NY 55
DYEN, Don (Illus), Newtown, PA 201
EBERT,Len(Illus), Douglasville, PA 200
EMBER, Kathy (Illus), Fleetwood, PA 125
ETTLINGER, Doris (Illus), Hampton, NJ....240
GARROW, Dan (Illus), Wilmington, DE 28
GLAZER, Art (Illus), Mt. Kisco, NY....246
GOLD, Marcy (Illus), Monticello, NY 262
GROTE, Rich (Illus), Hamilton Square, NJ....17
GYURCSAK, Joe (Illus), Mercerville, NJ 162
GYURCSAK, Lisa (Rep), Mercerville, NJ....162
HAEFELE, Steve (Illus), Mahopac, NY 96
HARDEN, Laurie (Illus), Boonton Twp, NJ 268
HERGERT, Greg (Illus), Morris Plains, NJ 66
ISKOWITZ, Joel (Illus), Woodstock, NY....209
KEETER, Susan (Illus), Syracuse, NY....130
KROVATIN, Daniel (Illus), Trenton, NJ 178
MACNEILL, Scott (Illus), Lambertsville, NJ....243
O'MALLEY, Kevin (Illus), Baltimore, MD 191
PALMER, Jan (Illus), North River, NY 123
ROBERTS, Scott (Illus), Baltimore, MD 86
ROPER, Robert (Illus), Philadelphia, PA 34
TURK, Melissa (Rep), Suffern, NY 188-191
VELORIC, Philip M. (Rep), Broomall, PA 199-205

SOUTH (AL AR FL GA KY LA MS NC OK SC TN TX VA)

CLARK, Michael (Des), Richmond, VA 287
CLEMENT, Cameron (Illus), Tulsa, OK....46
COOLEY, Rick (Illus), Check, VA....205
ERICKSON, Richard (Illus), Rydal, GA....129
GALEY, Chuck (Illus), Jackson, MS 68
GAMBLE, Kent (Illus), Lubbock, TX....145
GRAVES, Linda (Illus), Chesapeake, VA....215
HANNON, Holly (Illus), Greenville, SC 100
HARTER, Jim (Illus), San Antonio, TX 63
HOBBS, Bill (Illus), Greensboro, NC....106
LADEN, Nina (Illus), Atlanta, GA 160

LESTER, Mike (Illus), Rome, GA 40,41
LOVELL, Rick (Illus), Alpharetta, GA 14
MACKECHNIE, Anne V. (Des), Lexington, KY 284
MANTHA, Nancy (Illus), Austin, TX 211
MCCANN CO., The (Rep), Dallas, TX 145
MCCLURE, Tim (Illus), Dallas, TX 52
PIERRE, Keith (Des), N. Lauderdale, FL 275
PUNCHATZ, Don Ivan (Illus), Arlington, TX 20
REPERTOIRE/Andrea Lynch (Rep), Dallas, TX 68
SALEM, Kay (Illus), Houston, TX 53
SANDS, Trudy (Rep), Dallas, TX 51-53
SOPER, Pat (Illus), Lafayette, LA 180
TAGEL, Peggy (Illus), Dallas, TX 128
THE WRITE DIRECTION (Des), Athens, GA 276
THOMPSONS, The (Illus), Greenville, SC 104
WOLEK, Guy (Illus), Broken Arrow, OK 58
YALOWITZ, Paul (Illus), Palm Harbor, FL 113
YERKES, Lane (Illus), Fort Myers, FL 199

MIDWEST (IL IN IA KS MO MN NE ND OH SD WI)

ADAMS, Cheryl O. (Des), DesMoines, IA 278
BAHM, Bob (Rep), Cleveland, OH 20
BUTLER DESIGNER SIGN CO. (Des), Syracuse, IN 286
FLOCK ILLUSTRATION (Illus), Riverside, IL 43
KENNEDY, Anne (Illus), Galena, OH 126
KUCHARSKI, Michael (Illus), Wyandotte, MI 111
O'MALLEY, Kathleen (Illus), Chicago, IL 179
ROBINSON, Anthony Valentino (Illus), Garfield, OH 22
ROSALES, Melodye (Illus), Chicago, IL 101
SILVERS, Bill (Illus), Westlake, OH 118
STATON, Margaret (Illus), Allegan, MI 213
TAYLOR, B.K. (Illus), Franklin, MI 69
THOMPSON, Darren (Illus), Anderson, IN 239

WEST (AK AZ CA CO HI ID MT NV NM OR UT WA WY)

ABRAMS, Edward (Illus), Julian, CA 59
AMICOSANTE, Vincent (Illus), Capitola, CA 85
BERNARDIN, James (Illus), Edmonds, WA 35
BJORKMAN, Steve (Illus), Irvine, CA 31
DEAL, Jim (Illus), Seattle, WA 94
FREDRICKSON, Mark (Illus), Tucson, AZ 24,25
FUJISAKI, Tuko (Illus), San Diego, CA 115
GEARY, Rick (Illus), San Diego, CA 60
GREGER, C. Shana (Illus), Placitas, NM 216
GROSSMAN, Myron (Illus), Pasadena, CA 83
JOHNSON, Iskra (Des), Seattle, WA 277
JOHNSON, Larry (Illus), Placenta, CA 177
KAY DESIGN, Laura (Des), Ashland, OR 282
MICHAELS, Serge (Illus), N. Hollywood, CA 84,251
MUELCHI, Jannine (Illus), Carlsbad, NM 114
NIKOSEY, Tom (Des/Illus), Bell Canyon, CA 222,223
OLIMB GRAFIX (Illus), San Diego, CA 78,266
REINHARDT, Dorothy (Illus), San Francisco, CA 64
SANO, Kazuhiko (Illus), Mill Valley, CA 29
SCROGGY, David (Rep), San Diego, CA 59-61
SPENGLER, Ken (Illus), Sacramento, CA 56,57
SWENY, Stephen (Illus), Venice, CA 71
TALARO, Lionel (Illus), San Diego, CA 61
VEROUGSTRAETE, Randy (Illus), Spring Valley, CA 127
WALDMAN, Bryna (Illus), Ashland, OR 206

FRANCE

LEMANT, Albert (Illus), Bains 131

GREAT BRITAIN

GOFFE, Toni (Illus), Alton 214
HOLDER, John (Illus), Cambridge 204
SOURS, Michael (Illus), Oxford, England 51

WHAT IS CALLBACK®?

IF YOU'RE HAVING TROUBLE CONTACTING AN ARTIST IN RSVP, USE CALLBACK, OUR 24 HR., 7 DAY A WEEK, ANSWERING SERVICE. WE MAINTAIN DATABASE RECORDS OF ALL CHANGES OF ADDRESS AND PHONE NUMBER FOR PARTICIPATING ARTISTS. OUR STAFF RECEIVES YOUR CALL, RELAYS YOUR MESSAGE AND KEEPS A RUNNING RECORD OF ALL YOUR REFERRALS.

BACK EDITIONS

EACH ANNUAL EDITION OF RSVP FEATURES A COMPLETELY DIFFERENT SPECTRUM OF ARTISTS AND ARTWORK. BACK EDITIONS ARE AVAILABLE AT SPECIALLY REDUCED PRICES. ALL COPIES ARE BRAND NEW. QUANTITIES ARE LIMITED AND SOME EDITIONS ARE ALREADY OUT OF PRINT, SO PLEASE CONTACT US IMMEDIATELY FOR ORDERING INFORMATION.

TO ADVERTISE IN RSVP:

ANY ILLUSTRATOR, DESIGNER, PHOTOGRAPHER OR REP WANTING TO BE PLACED ON OUR MAILING LIST FOR INFORMATION ABOUT PAGE RATES, DEADLINES, ETC. IS ENCOURAGED TO CONTACT US AT 718/857-9267 OR RSVP: THE DIRECTORY OF CREATIVE TALENT, P.O. BOX 314, BROOKLYN, NEW YORK 11205